TEACHER-THERAPIST

This book is part of the Goodyear Series in Education,
Theodore W. Hipple, Editor
University of Florida

OTHER GOODYEAR BOOKS IN GENERAL METHODS & CENTERS

AH HAH! *The Inquiry Process of Generating and Testing Knowledge*
John McCollum

A CALENDAR OF HOME/SCHOOL ACTIVITIES
Jo Anne Patricia Brosnahan and Barbara Walters Milne

CHANGE FOR CHILDREN *Ideas and Activities for Individualizing Learning*
Sandra N. Kaplan, Jo Ann B. Kaplan, Sheila K. Madsen, Bette K. Taylor

CREATING A LEARNING ENVIRONMENT *A Learning Center Handbook*
Ethel Breyfogle, Susan Nelson, Carol Pitts, Pamela Santich

THE LEARNING CENTER BOOK *An Integrated Approach*
Tom Davidson, Phyllis Fountain, Rachel Grogan, Verl Short, Judy Steely, Katherine Freeman

ONE AT A TIME ALL AT ONCE *The Creative Teacher's Guide to Individualized*
Instruction Without Anarchy
Jack Blackburn and Conrad Powell

OPEN SESAME *A Primer in Open Education*
Evelyn M. Carswell and Darrell L. Roubinek

THE OTHER SIDE OF THE REPORT CARD *A How-to-Do-It Program*
for Affective Education
Larry Chase

THE TEACHER'S CHOICE *Ideas and Activities for Teaching Basic Skills*
Sandra N. Kaplan, Sheila K. Madsen, Bette T. Gould

TEACHING FOR LEARNING *Applying Educational Psychology in the Classroom*
Myron H. Dembo

OTHER WAYS, OTHER MEANS *Altered Awareness Activities for Receptive Learning*
Alton Harrison and Diann Musial

WILL THE REAL TEACHER PLEASE STAND UP? *A Primer in Humanistic*
Education, 2nd edition
Mary Greer and Bonnie Rubinstein

A YOUNG CHILD EXPERIENCES *Activities for Teaching and Learning*
Sandra N. Kaplan, Jo Ann B. Kaplan, Sheila K. Madsen, Bette T. Gould

For information about these, or Goodyear books in Language Arts, Reading,
Science, Math, and Social Studies write to

Janet Jackson
Goodyear Publishing Company
1640 Fifth Street
Santa Monica, CA 90401
(213) 393-6731

TEACHER-THERAPIST
A Text-Handbook for Teachers of
EMOTIONALLY IMPAIRED CHILDREN

Doris Burkett Mosier and Ruth Burkett Park

Goodyear Publishing Company, Inc., Santa Monica, California

Library of Congress Cataloging in Publication Data

MOSIER, DORIS BURKETT.
    Teacher-therapist.

    Bibliography: p. 149
    Includes index.
        1. Mentally ill children—Education—Handbooks,
    manuals, etc.   2. Child psychopathology—Handbooks,
    manuals, etc.   3. Teacher-participation in personnel
    service—Handbooks, manuals, etc.   I. Park, Ruth
    Burkett, joint author.   II. Title.
LC4169.M67   371.9'4   79-751
ISBN 0-87620-889-8

Copyright ©1979 by
Goodyear Publishing Company, Inc.
Santa Monica, California 90401

Current printing (last number):

10   9   8   7   6   5   4   3   2

ISBN: 0-87620-889-8
Y-8898-2

Book and cover design: Don and Debra McQuiston
Composition and Art Production: Boyer & Brass, Inc.
Production Editor: Hal Humphrey

To the memory of a master teacher

our grandfather,
MILES PERES MORTON (1875–1968)

CONTENTS

Preface   ix

1   Introduction   1
What Is Emotional Impairment?   3
Underlying Causes of Emotional Impairment   4
Main Task of a Teacher-Therapist   4
School Work as Therapy   4
Qualities Necessary to a Teacher-Therapist   5
What We've Said   6

2   The Classroom   7
Location and Arrangement   9
Personnel   9
Enrichment of Environment   10
Teaching Aids   10
Desk Arrangement   12
Classroom Atmosphere   12

3   Goals   13
Recording of Goals   16
Student Conferences   16
Short-Term Goals   17
Working for Goals   18
Daily Check Sheets   19
Overall Evaluations and Reports   21

4   Discipline   23
Teaching Self-Discipline   25
Actualization vs. Manipulation   27

The Democratic Classroom   29
Rules for Students   29
Rules for Teacher   30
Consistency   30
Principle of Controlled Freedom   31
Modeling and Role-Playing   32
Self-Discipline for Teacher   33

5   Aggressive Behaviors   35
Clowning   37
Teasing and Bullying   38
Tattling   40
Nagging   41
Hostility   41
Temper Tantrums   42

6   Passive Behaviors   45
Withdrawn Behaviors   47
Autism   48
Masturbation   53
Clumsiness   53
Stuttering   54

7   Deceptive Behaviors   55
Untruthfulness   57
Pathological Lying   58
Stealing   59
Cheating   61
Developing Trust   63

**8   Behaviors Stemming from Physical
Impairment**   65
Combining Objectivity and Support   67
Hearing Impairment   69
Speech Impairment   69
Blindness   70
Blindisms   71
Partial Visual Impairment   71
Learning Disability   72
Educable Mentally Impaired Children   72
Hyperactivity   73
Epilepsy   74
Brain Damage   75
Cerebral Palsy   75
Conclusion: Let Them Grow   76

**9   Teaching Reading, Spelling,
and Writing**   77
Types of Deficiencies   79
First Step in Remediation   80
Reading Instruction   81
Reciprocal Teaching   83
Relationships Between Spelling and Writing   83
Spelling and Writing Instruction   85

**10   Teaching Math, Science, and
Social Studies**   91
Mathematics   93
Science   96
Social Studies   98

11   Communicating with the Family   101
Cooperative Parents   103
Hostile Parents   104
Parent Conferences   107
Check Sheets at Home   107
Teaching a Double Standard   108

12   Grades, Checklists, and Reports   111
Grading in Special Classrooms   113
Evaluation of Behaviors   115
Reports to Parents   116
Reports from Parents   117
Bus Check Sheets   118
Check Sheets During Phasing Out   118

13   Token Economy   121
What Is Token Economy?   124
Answers to Criticisms of Token Economy   125
General Classroom Procedures   126
Rules for Using Tokens   127
Fines   130
Phasing Out of Tokens   131
Rewards   132
Stocking the Class Store   132
Privileges as Rewards   132
Sampling Rewards   133
Store Time   133
Setting Up an Economy   133
Rewarding Phase-Out Students   133
Risk and Advantages of Token Economy   134

14   Phasing Out and Screening Out   137
Phasing Out Begins on Day One   141
Use of Incremental Steps in Phasing Out   142
Prerequisites to Practice Phasing Out   143
The Final Phase: Screening Out   145
Follow-up   146

Suggested Reading for Teachers   147
Suggested Reading for Parents   148
Bibliography   149
Index   150

PREFACE

Of all the pupils at the knight school Gawaine le Coeur-Hardy was among the least promising. He was tall and sturdy, but his instructors soon discovered that he lacked spirit. He would hide in the woods when the jousting class was called, although his companions and members of the faculty sought to appeal to his better nature by shouting to him to come out and break his neck like a man. Even when he was told that the lances were padded, the horses no more than ponies, the field usually soft for late autumn, Gawaine refused to grow enthusiastic. The Headmaster and Assistant Professor of Pleasaunce were discussing the case one spring afternoon, and the Assistant Professor could see no remedy but expulsion.

"No," said the Headmaster, as he looked out at the purple hills which ringed the school, "I think I'll train him to slay dragons."

"He might be killed," objected the Assistant Professor.

"So he might," replied the Headmaster brightly; "but," he added more soberly, "we must consider the greater good. We are responsible for the formation of this lad's character." *

HEYWOOD BROUN, *The Fifty-First Dragon*

*Heywood Broun, ''The Fifty-First Dragon,'' in *Studies in the Short Story*, eds. Julian L. Maline and James Berkley, Approaches to Literature, vol. 1 (New York: Singer/Random House, 1969), pp.117–125.

Newly accredited educators frequently discover that being placed suddenly in full charge of a classroom brings uneasy confrontation with circumstances never mentioned in college courses. Even the required student teaching experience fails to prepare a fledgling teacher for the limitless variety of differences in children—and the unforeseen complexities that arise in any school setting.

If this statement is true for the average first-year teacher, it applies more acutely to anyone who is setting out to assume the role of teacher-therapist for children bearing the diagnosis, "emotionally impaired." This book is addressed to aspiring teacher-therapists of elementary classes for emotionally impaired children. Although it offers a number of definite techniques for dealing with youngsters who have been thus designated, it cannot presume to cover typical cases, since no individual is typical. Therefore, the book's main goals are: (a) to set forth a general description of conditions a teacher-therapist can expect to encounter; (b) to discuss some practical methods for approaching various problems; (c) to suggest a set of classroom procedures that can help a teacher maintain consistent management of day-to-day challenges; and (d) to encourage every teacher to develop flexibility and originality within the framework of a broadly determined philosophy.

Flexibility and originality cannot be overrated. Since no two children—whatever their academic or psychological designations—are alike, it is essential that a teacher be alert to recognize each student's unique reactions to environmental factors. On becoming aware of conditions that elicit positive reactions from a child, as well as of circumstances that are apt to trigger negative emotional outbursts from him, a teacher can find efficient ways to serve that child's best interests.

However, one trait all individual students have in common is that they respond to attention—in one way or another—and this is the crux of any teacher's influence. The teacher-therapist's principal objective should be to provide the kinds of attention that embrace (a) mutual understanding of goals that are desirable to both the student and the teacher; (b) teacher leadership in routines that make progress toward these stated goals; and (c) provision for individual originality and appropriate self-expression.

The danger in adopting a set of rigidly established classroom techniques lies in the obvious fact that each teacher also is unique. There is a tendency for any system to become ineffective—a sterile ritual—unless room is made in it for input from the teacher's unique intelligence and personality. The following quotation illustrates.

> It was . . . difficult to get rid of a student Lovaas had sent over to our house to help put Noah through his paces at home. In that case Noah's fate had to be tied into academic rigmarole. The student was arrogant, smug, seemed more inclined to punish Noah than reward him. When I told him I thought we could do without him he was crushed. "You don't understand," he said, "Noah is very important to me. He means six credits." Finally I had to prevail upon Lovaas, in his role of professor, to assign other "research projects" to this particular student.
>
> And Lovaas is primarily involved in a research project on the utilization of conditioning techniques as therapeutic tools. But he himself is a virtuoso therapist. On the occasions he has "worked" with Noah he has been a marvel and a revelation to observe–always firm but affectionate, strong yet loving. He has been able to elicit responses out of Noah–the repetition of sounds, for example–that no one else can. His students–or disciples–are all stiff and derivative compared to him. For the tough-treatment approach obviously derives from a gentle-hearted man who can thus in a sense "play the patient" with the skill of a classically trained musician hip to all the joys of jazz improvisation.[1]

Not everyone can expect to become a gifted teacher or teacher-therapist. However, it is altogether likely that most cases of inadequate classroom results occur because of the teacher's lack of courage to use original thinking—not because of laziness or incompetence.

A framework or so-called philosophy of teaching is essential; so is a supply of learned procedures for its implementation. But equally essential are a constant readiness to react to new situations with self-assured openness and a willingness to learn from students through interacting with them.

Preparation of these chapters involved a semantic dilemma that sprang from the unfortunate fact that there are a limited number of ways a writer can refer to individuals in a species that contains two genders. On the pedagogical side, the risk of being called sexist was nicely sidestepped

1. Josh Greenfeld, *A Child Called Noah* (New York: Warner Paperback Library, 1973). Copyright ©1970, 1971, 1972 by Josh Greenfeld. Reprinted by permission of Holt, Rinehart and Winston, Publishers.

when it was decided to address you, the reader (and assumedly the prospective teacher) directly.

When it came to writing about students, however, a problem loomed. The choices were simple, but appalling from the literary viewpoint. They were as follows:

1. Intersperse the words *student, youngster, kid* (?), *pupil, boy* or *girl, lad, lass,* and other possible synonyms for *child*. This threatened to yield examples such as: "At the end of the day, each child's behavior can be evaluated with the student's help. Since the youngster knows the kid's own problem areas, it is appropriate to ask the pupil . . ."

2. Giving careful thought to equal treatment, use the personal pronouns denoting both sexes. Then the same example would read: "At the end of the day, each child's behavior can be evaluated with her or his help. Since he or she knows her or his own problem areas, it is appropriate to ask him or her to evaluate her or his own behavior."

Admittedly, these illustrations are exaggerated; nevertheless they point to the enigma faced by any user of the language who wishes to circumvent stereotyped biases that are intrinsic to clear English sentences. Short of adopting newly coined inclusive pronouns such as *ne, ner* and *nis*—which are not only jarringly strange but also fail to solve the question satisfactorily—the only remaining course was to fall back on a conventional usage of male-oriented terms to designate both male and female beings.

A quotation to support this policy appears below. It is taken (out of context) from a dissertation that decries the male prejudices built into language, but which fails to suggest a way out of the predicament.

But the avoidance of sexist bias does not require tampering with hallowed terms by using stilted and artificial forms. A decent sense of English style wed to genuine regard for the dignity and equality of both sexes will produce good writing without either sexist bias or artificial distortions.

Some linguists may point out, as did Jacques Barzun in a recent issue of the Columbia Forum, *that* man *in its distant etymological past really meant "human" and that in its compounds, such as* mankind, *does properly include males and females alike. According to these linguists, it is being pointlessly, and indeed incorrectly, finicky to seek to avoid the generic use of male terms. . . ."* [2]

2. Dan Macy, "Men's Words: Women's Roles," *Saturday Review*, 14 June 1975, p. 57. Reprinted by permission of *Saturday Review.*

To J. Eric Hayes, whose criticisms and suggestions have been invaluable in preparation of the manuscript, the authors extend heartfelt thanks. In addition, we are grateful to Dr. Edsel Erickson, Ruth Rogers Erickson, Martha Neumann, and Charles Burkett for their advice and encouragement; to Robert P. Hawkins and Richard W. Malott for their influence in shaping the ideas in this book; and to Barbara McFadden for her help with typing and other important details.

TEACHER-THERAPIST

1
INTRODUCTION

Dear Miss Landers: My brother telephoned me last night, quite upset. His son Jerry, who is six years old and in the first grade, is known for picking on the other kids and makes a general nuisance of himself. The principal warned him that if Jerry hasn't settled down by the time school starts in the fall, he will be expelled.

Is it possible to expel a first grader? How can Jerry be helped?

—Concerned Uncle

Dear Uncle: A child whose anti-social behavior disrupts the classroom can be expelled no matter what his age. . . .[1]

---

1. Ann Landers, in *Kalamazoo Gazette*, 14 July 1975. Copyright 1975 by Field Newspaper Syndicate, Chicago. Reprint permission granted by Ann Landers.

The foregoing quotation demonstrates that, as late as 1975, awareness of federal education laws was sadly lacking in this country. In current years of burgeoning special education programs, countless otherwise knowledgeable persons remain unaware of the fact that no child in the United States, regardless of his physical, mental, or emotional handicaps, can be denied a public education. Federal law protects the rights of all children in this regard. It also makes funds available to every state for education and training of the impaired. An increasing number of states are establishing special education classes for children having specific handicaps, with the express purpose of preparing them to function successfully in regular classrooms. This trend has given the category of handicap termed *emotional impairment* full status in the special education curriculum.

WHAT IS EMOTIONAL
IMPAIRMENT?

A youngster who has been diagnosed emotionally impaired is one who has been designated, by a professional assessment team including a psychologist and a social worker, as an individual who exhibits behaviors that make it difficult or impossible for him to perform acceptably in a regular classroom situation.

In a district offering special education services, a teacher, on identifying such a child, confers with the school principal and the student's parents as early as possible. A request-for-special-education-services form, containing a short summary of the child's inappropriate behaviors, is signed by one parent and the teacher or principal for forwarding to the school psychologist. Since disruptive and other unusual behaviors sometimes stem from physical causes, psychologists frequently request further examination by physicians, neurologists, or specialists in visual or hearing problems and other impairments.

When the student enters your class, his cumulative file shows a general description of his behaviors, the diagnostic findings, and a set of behavior goals the child must meet to function in a conventional classroom.

UNDERLYING
CAUSES OF
EMOTIONAL
IMPAIRMENT

Reasons for a child's acquisition of the label *emotional impairment* are numerous and diverse. Whatever they may be, the teacher's primary concern is the presence of maladaptive behavior and/or the absence of appropriate behavior. This is not to imply that origins of such behavior are not important; but since no teacher can change what has happened to a child in the past, you must accept the student as he is and start relating to him in the current moment. As Will Rogers once commented, "If a snake bites you, you ain't going to stop and study out where he come from and why he was there at the time; you want to start figuring out what to do right then."

Although attitudes and feelings are vital, they cannot be dealt with directly; behaviors can be. The ways a child acts allow speculation about his inner feelings, but any change of those inner feelings is measurable only through observation of altered behavior.

MAIN TASK OF A
TEACHER-THERAPIST

The main task of a teacher-therapist is to help children learn to substitute socially appropriate academic and social behaviors and attitudes for practices that previously excluded them from the academic mainstream. You'll be expected to guide each youngster to recognition of his long-term goals; to help him determine criteria for a series of short-term goals that lead to success; and to work with him toward achieving that success.

During the course of your working with him, clues concerning his past experiences inevitably come to your attention. Also, you may notice conditions needing further medical analysis or intervention in the home by health authorities. Details that come to light, combined with material in the child's school records, can provide much insight into his basic emotional structure and help you find direction in guiding him academically and in his interpersonal relationships.

SCHOOL WORK AS
THERAPY

Your role as teacher of the emotionally impaired is exactly what it implies: the dual function of (1) helping students to improve their academic skills to the extent of their individual capacities and (2) helping them to substitute appropriate behaviors for inappropriate ones.

Schoolwork is an ideal vehicle for achieving this dual responsibility, since it allows objectivity in dealing with children and furnishes constant interpersonal contact simultaneously. Learning experiences that are interesting, challenging, and within a child's ability level have proved to be therapeutic in themselves. Since learning involves facts and the majority of emotionally impaired children have had past difficulty in assimilating facts at least partially because of behaviors that have inhibited their learning processes, you use facts as a basic ingredient in therapy.

The facts themselves serve a three-fold function. First, they can be used to catch interest and attention; second, they can provide the means by which you and the child progress in accomplishing desired behavioral changes; and third, they add to the child's knowledge and resulting self-assurance.

Consequently, the factual material learned by an emotionally impaired child is significant, not just to the school system and to you as his teacher, but to the child himself. Any measure of school success adds to his self-confidence and results in improved relationships with others. Thus, through meeting a series of short-term academic and behavioral goals, the child becomes equipped to fulfill the primary long-term goal: his return to a regular classroom.

QUALITIES
NECESSARY TO A
TEACHER-THERAPIST

Some techniques that have proved effective in teaching emotionally impaired children are presented in following chapters. No set rule, pattern, or method can be guaranteed to cure any particular condition. The success of whatever technique you decide to employ with any given child depends on your own implementation of that technique, plus your willingness to modify it to fit the needs of that child.

Techniques are merely tools handled with varying degrees of expertise and sensitivity. Expertise comes with practice—but, when you're dealing with the emotionally impaired, practice fails to develop expertise unless it is accompanied at all times by sensitivity and objectivity.

It can be assumed that you already possess sensitivity or you wouldn't have chosen the field of special education; but to use properly your ability to respond to the behavior of an emotionally impaired child, your response must be governed by intellectual judgment. You may empathize deeply with the wounded feelings of a disturbed child but realize that either commiseration or a reprimand might result in reinforcement of the inappropriate behavior with which the child is expressing those feelings. On the other hand you may be tempted to take it personally when a student's emotions get out of hand and he lashes out against you or expresses deep hurt because of something you did (or failed to do). Objective control at such times is imperative. The time to discuss whatever precipitated an inappropriate behavior is after the emotional storm has passed, when you can talk to the child calmly and expect him to be more objective. On occasions when you have been wrong—and you won't always be right—later is also the time to show your honesty and respect for him as a person by making an appropriate apology.

The ensuing chapters present some concrete examples of demonstrated ways that emotionally disturbed children have been taught and guided in classroom situations. After reading this book, you should be prepared to go forth as a teacher-therapist armed with something more than vague notions of theoretical constructs that try to explain the intrapsychic dynamics of emotional impairment; you'll also possess some definite ideas concerning *what to do*.

WHAT WE'VE SAID   1. From the standpoint of society, the emotionally impaired child is *behaviorally* impaired.

2. The function of a teacher-therapist is to provide academic learning and, simultaneously, teach each child to substitute socially acceptable behaviors (the outward indicators of attitudes and feelings) for those that previously excluded him from regular classrooms, so the child can return to a regular classroom.

3. The success of any technique a teacher uses depends on (a) the teacher's willingness to modify it to meet the needs of the individual student; (b) expertise in the use of techniques, which comes with practice; and (c) the teacher's sensitivity, which must be tempered by objective judgment.

2
THE CLASSROOM

Classroom corners—stale and pale!
Classroom corners—cobweb covered!
Teacher, let me dance in your classroom corner!
Let the outside world in! [1]

ALBERT CALLUM, *The Geranium on the Window Sill Just*
Died But Teacher You Went Right On

1. Albert Callum, *The Geranium on the Window Sill Just Died But Teacher You Went Right On* (New York: Harlan Quist, 1971), p. 10. Reprinted by permission of the publisher.

Bearing in mind that your students will be preparing for eventual return to regular classrooms, you should maintain a setting for their learning experiences that is as conventional as possible. Whatever modifications you employ should logically accommodate the services of a special education room, but modifications need not be drastic.

LOCATION AND
ARRANGEMENT

Knowledgeable school administrators are aware that special education students deserve facilities equal to those furnished in regular classrooms. Occasionally, however, it becomes necessary for a special education teacher to bring this fact to administrative attention. Many states have guidelines for the operation of special school programs, which spell out criteria concerning room size, square feet per desk, lighting, and other necessities, with explicit provision for financial reimbursement to the district. Some administrators, although following the guidelines, practice segregation by assigning rooms in isolated areas of the school to special education; others seem to regard special education rooms as supplementary and give them the least convenient space in the building. Even the practice of scheduling special education students for separate lunch and recess periods has occurred.

If you are given a room that segregates your class or that fails to conform to standards met by other classrooms, it would be advisable for you to investigate your state's special education laws. Then find out who in your district is responsible for assigning classrooms and pursue a tactful means of calling the matter to that person's attention. This is not to suggest that you become belligerent in any way.

If there are no results after you have done all you can to change the situation, adjust to it temporarily. When the results of your work with students become apparent, the value of your classroom will be evident and you'll be in a stronger position to request better facilities.

PERSONNEL

A classroom for children who have been diagnosed emotionally impaired should employ the services of at least one teacher's aide. Ideally, because of the necessity to give students a great deal of individual attention, class size should be limited to ten or twelve, and there should be three supervising adults. Assistants to the teacher might be a student instructor and an aide or two aides, at least one of whom is a student in educational psychology, special education, or a related field.

As a matter of fact, every candidate for the profession of teaching in a special education classroom should be required to serve a semester's field placement as a routine part of each year's curriculum, assisting a special education teacher. In addition to supplying reliable teacher assistants economically, this arrangement would provide special education students with direct supervised experience in preparation for their future work. Special education students involved in operating classrooms could then offer feedback to the university regarding which parts of its special education course work are relevant to actual performance and which are not. (This process would appear to be feasible for regular education as well.)

Whatever the arrangement, every adult supervisor must be thoroughly acquainted with room procedures. Each adult should also know every student's academic level, behavioral habits, and current achievement status in relation to goals. This enables you and your helpers to maintain consistency in working with the class and with each child. It also makes it possible for you to depend on efficient fulfillment of daily lesson plans, in case one adult has to be absent, without interrupting any student's program.

ENRICHMENT OF ENVIRONMENT

Unfortunately, the notion that classrooms for emotionally impaired children should be bare and unstimulating (to avoid distractions) has been accepted by some educators. This idea is illogical. Even if a monotonous physical environment could reduce emotional stimulation, such surroundings would defeat their own purpose. Your aim is to help children fit into normal situations; you don't prepare restless students to cope with distractions by placing them in a vacuum, but by showing them how to use stimuli for development of learning and behavioral skills. Length of attention span in the classroom depends less on extraneous surroundings than on teaching techniques.

Accordingly, you should provide a classroom setting that is as attractive as possible to help your students gain appreciation for an interesting environment and take pride in their room. Expect them to share cleaning up chores, and sponsor the attitude, "We live here most of every day and we want it to look pleasant—not just for visitors but also for us."

TEACHING AIDS

Art displays and science projects should be changed frequently. Items such as an aquarium, a terrarium, and small animals and plants that must be cared for can provide responsibilities for students; and a bulletin board that is altered or renewed regularly should be considered an on-going class project.

Bulletin boards displaying contributions from every student establish that important visual aid as an extension of the learning process. Teacher-made bulletin boards, although often impressive and more attractive than those made by children, involve the interests of a class much less than those the students take part in constructing. You can help your class select general topics and plans for bulletin boards, but encourage the students to participate in building them.

Copies of good paintings, pop art, and pictures of outstanding people (contemporary as well as historic), cut from magazines and rotated as wall decorations, furnish topics for discussion. Start with pictures you know to be of interest to at least one member of the class, then proceed to subjects that can broaden the students' knowledge and interests.

Because of the spread of age, grade, and ability level in students diagnosed as emotionally impaired, choose the most varied supply of reading materials you can acquire for your room's library. Additional books should be readily accessible from the school library or resource center.

No textbook is more than a teaching tool; in classes where individual differences are pronounced, it is a grave mistake to adopt a single textbook series. Insist on freedom to select materials relevant to each student's needs—including workbooks and drill sheets, many of which provide only busywork and actually don't teach anything. After each child has reduced his educational deficiencies, he'll be amenable to the reintroduction of regular textbooks—a necessary step in preparing him for return to the educational mainstream.

Make sure that the standard audiovisual aids used in other classrooms are available to your room on an equal basis with all others. Tapes, records, films, and other attention-getting devices lend new dimensions to learning; use them often. Most youngsters especially enjoy recording stories of their own composition, then listening to their taped voices.

Activity centers like those used in open classrooms can provide constructive use of free time. These should be designated for art, science experiments, games, and other free-time interests, and they should be available only after students have accomplished assigned work with acceptable results. Students should be expected to state clearly one choice of activity for a specific period and to remain with it the full time. The total open classroom concept, although it might work with this type of special education student, is not advocated because of the amount of structure that would have to be built into it. Children with behavior irregularities need structure for their academic program; with the use of activity centers, even their free time is structured; *but* they have choices of working to earn free time or not plus choices of activities to pursue during earned free time.

The advantages of preserving consistency through utilization of structure is demonstrated by examples given in subsequent chapters; but it's important to understand that the word structure in this context does not imply regimentation. Rather, it refers to a carefully planned organization of limits on student behavior, within which the student can choose from an established set of alternatives.

DESK
ARRANGEMENT

If desks can be moved, arrange them in a half circle that enables the students to see one another, the teacher, and the chalkboard. This encourages a sense of unity and cooperation and allows desks to be placed far enough apart to ensure each student an area of privacy.

When desks are movable, children working together on the same subject can move their desks together to form a table between them. It is also helpful to have several tables in the room to use for individual or small group teaching when part of the class is occupied with something else and to furnish shared work areas without shifting desks.

CLASSROOM
ATMOSPHERE

When both setting and procedure are planned ahead of time, an atmosphere of orderly calm becomes part of the necessary structure. In short, a classroom for the emotionally impaired must have certain special features, and giving careful thought to its arrangement increases your opportunities to function effectively as a teacher-therapist.

The kind of classroom atmosphere you desire evolves as your students settle into daily routines based on your own consistent but flexible behaviors. The following chapters on goals and discipline offer suggestions for setting up a system of generally expected classroom procedures that can markedly influence your students' contributions to a serene and productive daily agenda.

3
GOALS

Two fixed ideas can no more coexist in the nature of morality than two bodies can occupy one and the same space in the physical world.

PUSHKIN

Your general long-term goal is already established: to help your students learn to replace inappropriate behaviors, which have caused them to be excluded from regular classrooms, with the appropriate behaviors they need for acceptance to the educational mainstream. The methods you use in achieving this sweeping goal consist largely of your getting to know each child, then setting a series of short-term goals that will lead that child through a series of steps to the ultimate objective.

Every student should come into your classroom with a set of specifically stated long-range goals that must be met to qualify the child for reentry to the mainstream (screening out into regular education). In many school systems these goals constitute the basis of a formally recorded and signed agreement between the referring parties (school and parents) and the receiving parties (special education division and teacher). Measurable objectives—both academic and behavioral—are prescribed by a psychologist or other professional who has examined and observed the child. They are formulated with the assistance of parents, the former teacher, and other professionals who know the child well.

A typical prescription might read, in part: "At the end of ninety days in the special class, Katie will use cursive handwriting 100 percent of the time. She will spell words at third-grade level with 80 percent accuracy and read silently without moving her lips at least 80 percent of the time. At the end of six months, she will score at least 70 percent in reading comprehension at third-grade level. . . . Behaviorally, by the end of the current school year, Katie will stay in her seat 95 percent of the time; remain quiet while others are talking 95 percent of the time; and she will have eliminated all tantrum behavior."

If such formalities aren't observed by your school system, it is your *first duty* to fix the goals each one of your students must meet before he can be considered ready to go back to a regular classroom. You can do this by studying the child's cumulative records and by conferring personally with his parents, former teacher, and other persons you know to be acquainted with the reasons for his referral to special education.

RECORDING OF
GOALS

Regardless of whether you're furnished with a formal prescription, you'll wish to arrive at a comprehensive view of each student's strengths and weaknesses by studying his or her records and gathering background information from other individuals. Based on this, write down a list of objectives for the student and keep it in a place where you can refer to it often.

The importance of establishing realistic, measurable goals in written record form cannot be overemphasized, because these are the yardsticks against which you measure each student's progress, and they are the ultimate standards the students must meet before they can return to a conventional classroom. Also, by recording an account of a child's progress (or lack of it) as measured by these goals, you provide an objective assessment that will prove vastly more accurate than any you could possibly reach through subjective judgment. (For example, a student might meet a certain behavioral goal 80 percent of the time, but, unless you are recording that fact, his 20 percent failure could be exaggerated in your subjective thinking; and the same could be true in reverse.)

STUDENT
CONFERENCES

Before setting up short-term, day-to-day goals, seek input from the persons most concerned with the overall concept of individual goals—the students themselves. Conferences to discuss each student's goals with him individually should take place as early in the school year as they can be arranged. Since student involvement is a crucial factor in guidance toward self-management, each student should be aware of the goals he is working for—and he *must* accept them. The student should also be asked for comments on what he believes to be his problem areas.

Approach the student with friendliness and courtesy, making it clear that you want to arrive at a mutual understanding of his problems and of behavior areas he would like to change. Tact is always in order, but there is no necessity to evade issues; students are fully aware of the implications of special education placement, and most of them know at least vaguely why they have been put in your room. Each conference could start with your telling the child about the goals that have been stated for him and asking for his comments. Additional goals suggested by him can be discussed; if you agree they are relevant, write them down, making sure each one is observable and measurable.

Explain to the student that special check sheets will be used to evaluate his progress, and tell him that he will be asked to help with the evaluations. Let him know you are on his side, enthusiastic about his desire to improve and confident in his chances for success; but emphasize that accomplishment of his goals will require sincere effort on his part as well as yours.

Few private conferences are needed after the initial one, because the youngsters tell each other about their goals, discuss their check sheets openly, and eventually begin to help one another by following examples you set in dealing with particular behaviors.

SHORT-TERM GOALS   A child is more likely to sustain interest in a long-term goal when it is broken down into steps providing a series of short-term goals. For example, a youngster in the habit of whining probably will not learn to substitute for his habit (by asking calmly for things he wants) if he is repeatedly commanded to stop whining. However, if that youngster is praised and/or rewarded each time he asks calmly for something he wants, he is inclined to continue the preferred behavior.

Asked why he had sought help in reading and study skills at the college level, Robert told his tutor: "When I was in grade school my dad promised me a baseball, bat, and mitt if I would get all A's on my report card. I never got all A's, so I didn't get the baseball stuff. When I was in high school, he promised me an expensive wristwatch if I'd graduate in the top ten percent of my class–and I didn't get the wristwatch because I failed to make the top ten. Now, he has promised me a car if I graduate from college–and by God I'm going to beat that old dude out of a car!"

At the outset, Robert's father had failed to help his elementary school son establish a realistic long-term goal. Instead of demanding all A's, he should have offered the boy the coveted baseball equipment if he would raise the marks for subjects in which he was receiving poor reports by one letter grade. He should have set a specific time for this to be achieved, such as from one semester report card to the next. Then he could have stimulated Robert to work for his long-term goal by rewarding improvement in daily grades, with coins dropped in a piggy bank toward purchase of the final reward, plus daily privileges or special snacks.

Additionally, as soon as Robert began to maintain a satisfactory grade in any one subject, monetary rewards could have been slightly increased and placed on a weekly basis in recognition of keeping a grade average at a high level. This procedure of (1) setting achievable goals and (2) using incremental rewards for steady short-range progress might even have resulted in Robert's finally achieving all A's.

The criticism that a reward system consists of baiting a child with pay for doing things he should be expected to do anyway is unrealistic, since the reward system is intrinsic to our society. Most people expect financial compensation for work and we typically crave material gain, enjoyable vacations, and praise from the boss. The difference between most adults and children is that maturity develops ability to wait for a pay check at the end of the month, a Christmas bonus, or a semester grade. Adults can work long periods to save money for a new wardrobe or a trip to Europe; children generally need step-by-step encouragement.

The mother of two boys, seven and eight years of age, was distraught because she was unable to stop them from regular bed-wetting. She told the teacher of one son that she had tried every punishment and every method she knew of, but the boys continued to wet every night. She said she had considered offering new bunk beds to the pair as a reward for staying dry, but was afraid the new beds would be ruined. The teacher suggested putting the boys' spending money on an allowance basis by paying each one five cents on any morning his bed had not been wet. The mother accepted the idea; and between mid November and Christmas both boys had stopped wetting completely. They received the new bunk beds as a final reward for staying dry on fifteen consecutive nights.

In setting up classroom goals for students, answer the following questions for each student.

1. What is the end result desired, as agreed on by both teacher and student?

2. How can the end result be attained through a series of steps?

3. What are reasonable steps in terms of the individual child's capacity to sustain effort?

4. What criterion should be set for acceptable performance (50 percent and up, depending on the child's present behavior—see example prescription, p.15)?

5. What time limit should be allowed to achieve acceptable performance?

6. Does the child fully understand the goal and what he must do to reach it? Has he committed himself to these things?

WORKING FOR
GOALS

First of all, with the first short-term goals, make sure to reduce your expectations of performance to a minimal level to guarantee early success. In school subjects, start each child at a point at which he is comfortable with the material and can function without errors, then gradually increase the difficulty of tasks to provide continuous challenge until the first-step goal is reached. A second, more demanding goal can follow; and subsequent short-term aims should be designed to move the student steadily closer to his long-term goal.

Should a student get stuck at a learning plateau, apparently unable to progress beyond a given level, take time to analyze the situation and look for reasons.

Marian discovered that whenever she showed considerable effort in solving a math problem or thinking of an answer, her teacher would praise her for working hard and reward her efforts. Consequently Marian

*began to delay her responses, feigning deep concentration, and earning
rewards for accomplishing work at the same level over and over.
Knowing the child was able to progress, the teacher puzzled over the
situation until it became plain that Marian had learned to pretend she was
working hard so she could collect rewards. The teacher immediately
began to set time limits for Marian to come up with correct answers. She
withheld praise and rewards whenever the child's responses did not fall
within the specified time, and the problem was corrected in a single day.*

DAILY CHECK
SHEETS

Daily academic performance evaluations can be included in each student's check sheets, which also list the child's behavioral objectives. The student's name and space for the date appear at the top of each check sheet. On the left side, school subjects are listed and beneath those appear the youngster's individual behavior goals. To the right of these lists are three columns of spaces for marking symbols to indicate that day's performance level—good, fair, or try again. Sheets can be run off on a duplicating machine about once a month, which allows for possible changes in the list of behavior goals. The accompanying illustration is an example of one child's daily check sheet.

Assessments are entered at the end of each school day with the student, your adult helpers, and you participating in the evaluations.

Although all goal behaviors are appraised each day, it's advisable to ask each child to choose one target behavior to work on at a time. Usually the child agrees to commence with his most disruptive habit, giving special emphasis to substitution of an appropriate behavior. (Frequently, after one behavior has been singled out and its occurrence reduced, a youngster begins to generalize the improvement to other behaviors, because most behaviors in a single syndrome are interrelated.) A slip of paper bearing some reminder to the student of his current target behavior can be taped to his desk. This could be a cartoon or picture, a statement expressed in humorous or verse form, or some other symbol selected by the child.

Class business meetings are covered when we discuss the democratic classroom in chapter 4. These meetings encourage student input for formulation of general classroom behavior goals, and they tend to foster understanding and tolerance between individuals. Since rap sessions also establish standards of teacher behavior, you should share your own goals with the class and occasionally seek comments evaluating your progress.

By making check sheets a part of each day's ordinary routine and by bringing each individual's goals out for open scrutiny, you reduce students' anxieties by showing them that their classmates, too, have behavioral goals.

	Good	Fair	Try again
Elizabeth's CHECK SHEET FOR _Friday, March 14_			
Math		✓	
Reading	✓		
Spelling	✓		
Language		✓	
Social Studies	✓		
Handwriting			✓
I stayed in my seat at all appropriate times.	✓		
I talked only when called upon and/or during my turn.		✓	
I was friendly.	✓		
I worked independently until my work was finished.	✓		
I listened with others.		✓	
I used appropriate bathroom behavior.		✓	
I followed directions cheerfully.	✓		
I shared.		✓	
I handled learning and teaching materials appropriately.	✓		
I asked permission to leave the room.			✓
Parent comments:			
Parent signature			

A DAILY CHECK SHEET is completed in a brief conference with the student at the end of the school day. (Parent involvement should be dictated by individual circumstances.)

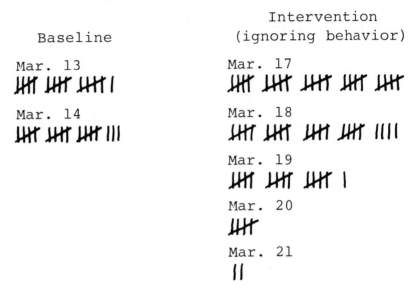

Diane, Instances of tattling

TALLY OF FREQUENCY OF A SPECIFIC BEHAVIOR gives an accurate count of observed instances of undesirable behavior. It measures the effectiveness of intervention being used in therapy and is used by the teacher in daily check-sheet conferences.

OVERALL
EVALUATIONS AND
REPORTS

The only way you can know whether or not a student is successfully meeting goals is to take data on a systematic basis. Keep a data sheet for each student recording his overall performance from his check sheets. This may appear at the outset to be time-consuming and unnecessary, but it is an essential part of your job. The teacher's data sheet provides an overview of a student's performance over a period of weeks or months. It summarizes information from the student's check sheet, reflecting general progress or lack of progress. It tells you at a glance whether or not the methods you are using are effective.

By recording one baseline that measures a student's academic achievement level and a separate baseline showing the frequency of his inappropriate behaviors, you establish bases of comparison for later checks. Not all student data sheets need be checked on the same day, but each should be done within a regular, periodic time frame of two to three months. Data sheets will give factual information on your students' rates of progress, more reliable than your own estimates. At times you may be surprised to discover that tabulated frequency of a behavior is much lower or higher than you expected it to be.

Finally, data sheets furnish accurate information for your official reports to the child, the home, consultants, and administrators; show you at the end of the school year whether or not your students have accom-

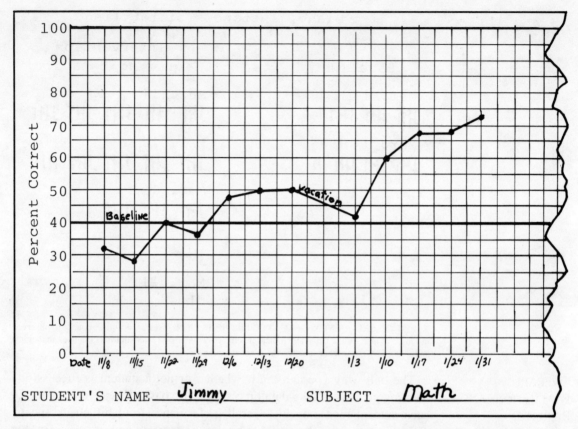

STUDENT'S NAME _____ *Jimmy* _____   SUBJECT _____ *Math* _____

OVERALL EVALUATION—Jimmy's prescription when he entered the special classroom called for raising his average math score from 40 per cent to 70 per cent by the end of the semester. Overall evaluation sheet reflects this student's weekly average math scores from November 8 to January 31 in relation to his original baseline average of 40 per cent.

plished their goals; point up areas that need modified planning; and provide general help in reevaluating students for setting the coming year's goals.

4
DISCIPLINE

April 23, 1663—At cards late, and being at supper, my boy being sent for some mustard to a neat's tongue, the rogue staid half an hour in the streets, it seems at a bonfire, at which I was very angry, and resolve to beat him tomorrow.

April 24, 1663—Up betimes, and with my salt eel went down to the parler and there got my boy and did beat him till I was fain to take breath two or three times, yet for all I am afeard it will make my boy never the better, he is grown so hardened in his tricks, which I am sorry for, he being capable of making a very brave man, and is a boy that I and my wife love very well.

THE DIARY OF SAMUEL PEPYS

Traditionally, the term *discipline* implies punitive action—an overt measure that aims to inflict suffering for wrongdoing and to prevent repetition (or imitation) of socially inappropriate behavior. Some students have experienced large overdoses of strict traditional discipline; others come from backgrounds of extreme permissiveness where virtually no limits were set on their behaviors. Still others are products of homes characterized by some mixture of disciplinary inconsistencies ranging from brutality to neglect.

Early in your first semester of teaching, you can guide such a heterogeneous group of emotionally impaired children in the development of new insights and self-disciplinary skills that will result in an orderly, productive classroom. The real purpose of discipline is to teach self-discipline. But any technique that aims to guide children toward self-discipline can be misused. One need look no further than the fiasco of progressive education, which was based on sound principles but failed in the hands of educators who did not understand that removal of authoritarianism would necessitate the substitution of some system of teaching self-discipline.

If it is to be learned, self-discipline (like anything else) must be practiced. Before they become willing to practice it, children must realize that it is valuable to them. While they are practicing it, they discover that it sets them free from outer restraints and adds to their feelings of self-worth.

TEACHING
SELF-DISCIPLINE

The first prerequisite to teaching self-discipline is to possess it yourself.

1. Maintain an objective attitude toward disruptive or withdrawing behaviors your students use to get your attention. Children are natural attention seekers. Although most youngsters are fortunate enough to learn in early years how to get attention by acting properly, it is deviant behavior that usually receives extraordinary attention in our society. News-

papers give a great deal of space to crime because readers show lively interest in unlawfulness, as well as in offenders.

2. Give attention to behaviors that are appropriate. Every time you praise a child for practicing the target behavior he is working on, or even look at him with approval to make him aware that you noticed, you encourage him to repeat that behavior.

Normal children may resist the authoritarian approach, but they are able to adjust to it most of the time. Although it often teaches them to regard fear of getting caught as more important than moral responsibility, they at least function within the system. On the other hand, emotionally or behaviorally impaired children are often overtly rebellious against authoritarianism. They have learned that refusal to conform gains them more attention than they get from being good. Thus they find ways to earn the aversive rewards frequently bestowed upon nonconformists by teachers, peers, and parents.

3. Remember that appropriate behavior and its diametrical opposite, inappropriate behavior, cannot take place at the same time. As a youngster learns to substitute appropriate behavior for behavior that is not appropriate, he learns to use self-discipline.

Suppose you are at the front of the room, giving directions to the class for an assignment. But Scott is out of his seat, sharpening his pencil, going from desk to desk, harrassing his classmates, and talking loudly about totally irrelevant subjects while you are attempting to hold class attention. Typically, you would say, "Scott, sit down. You may not be interested in the assignment, but you mustn't deprive the rest of the students of the chance to listen."

Scott's behavior continues; so you issue a sharp command for him to sit down. He might obey at this point—which would reinforce you as a disciplinarian—but after a few minutes he not only leaves his desk again but starts repeating the former behavior. You issue another firm command that Scott sit down; chances are, he will reinforce you again; and this procedure could be repeated as many as twenty times during the first hour of the day.

Meanwhile, Scott has not even made a first step toward learning to remain in his seat, simply because you have been training him to spring out of it with increasing frequency. He knows it will draw your attention and also cause every eye in the class to focus on him.

How can you reverse this process? Obviously, there is no instantaneous method; nevertheless, there is one that will, by progressive degrees, not only teach Scott to stay in his seat, but keep him there. Starting with the same situation, ignore Scott's disruptions until you can catch him in an instant of quiet, such as when he sits at his desk to get a pencil to sharpen.

If no such opportunity presents itself within the first five minutes, tell Scott firmly to sit down and wait for him to do it. Either way, when he is quiet reinforce the behavior *immediately* by saying pleasantly, "Thank you, Scott; now we can *all* take part in the class."

Continue to follow this procedure each time Scott leaves his seat. You will soon notice that the periods of time betwen his engaging in the behavior are lengthening. Finally, provided you remain consistent in ignoring disruptions, reinforcing him when he is quiet, and noticing children who are attentive, Scott will gradually begin to use the preferred behavior to elicit your attention and approval. Aided by his daily check sheet grades, and other reinforcements still to be discussed, this technique helps Scott to develop conscious self-discipline. As might be expected, this example is simplified to illustrate only the main elements of a situation. It's necessary for you to watch carefully the reactions of students until you get to know each individual. Occasionally a child becomes so upset when his misbehavior is ignored that the misbehavior snowballs until he lapses into a tantrum. You must be perceptive enough to nip this kind of reaction in the bud, probably by instituting some form of punishment. Take the child aside for a moment and make a deal with him, such as: "Each time you choose not to stay in your seat I will write down that you have lost five minutes free time at the activity center." When behaviors become totally disruptive to the work of the classroom, use a short period of isolation to give the offender time to vent his passions and become calm. If used sparingly and with empathy, isolation is a valuable tool in therapy.

Praise and attention for appropriate behavior can also bring undesirable effects, unless you take care to advance past the first stage of repeatedly reinforcing the same behavior. Repetition of reinforcement at the same level can result in teaching Scott to leave his seat more often to get attention for sitting down, if you do not—once you have him sitting— introduce praise for his staying quiet so as not to disturb the lesson, for listening to assignments, and finally for doing a good job (or trying hard) on an assignment. Comment on other children's quietness, attentiveness, and other appropriate behaviors at the same time as you are ignoring any disruptive behavior from Scott. This not only reinforces appropriate classroom behavior but tends to decrease peer attention to a disruptive student.

ACTUALIZATION VS. MANIPULATION

The reason any disciplinary procedure can fail when put into practice is that *no* procedure is effective if the person utilizing it considers it merely a mechanical means of reaching desired results. Before you adopt the techniques described here—or any other disciplinary system—you must be able to live that system, for its effectiveness necessarily depends on whether it is used superficially or with sincerity.

In other words, just as rewards can be misused in any kind of discipline, praise and attention used only as tools of manipulation are useless; even children who appear insensitive can spot the difference between true praise and the automatic mouthing of approving words. By the same token, the act of ignoring inappropriate behavior can become a form of cruelty; and a therapist who is emotionally incapable of becoming objective can easily lapse into impatience, threatening language, ridicule, and other behaviors that betray lack of self-discipline.

In his book, *Man, the Manipulator*, Everett L. Shostrom presents the following table to describe fundamental characteristics of manipulators in contrast to characteristics of people he calls actualizers. The distinctions it makes, although intended by the author to encompass all kinds of human relations, can be applied to any set of methods designed to achieve classroom discipline.[1]

MANIPULATORS

1. Deception (phoniness, knavery). The manipulator uses tricks, techniques, and maneuvers. He puts on an act, plays roles to create an *impression*. His expressed feelings are deliberately chosen to fit the occasion.

2. Unawareness (deadness, boredom). The manipulator is unaware of the really important concerns of living. He has tunnel vision. He sees only what he wishes to see and hears only what he wishes to hear.

3. Control (closed, deliberate). The manipulator plays life like a game of chess. He appears relaxed, yet is very controlled and controlling, concealing his motives from his "opponent."

4. Cynicism (distrust). The manipulator is basically distrusting of himself and others. Down deep he doesn't trust human nature. He sees relationships as having two alternatives: to control or *be* controlled.

ACTUALIZERS

1. Honesty (transparency, genuineness, authenticity). The actualizer is able honestly to be his feelings, whatever they may be. He is characterized by candidness, *expression*, and genuinely being himself.

2. Awareness (responsiveness, aliveness, interest). The actualizer fully listens to himself and others. He is fully aware of nature, art, music, and the other real dimensions of living.

3. Freedom (spontaneity, openness). The actualizer is spontaneous. He has the freedom to be and express his potentials. He is master of his life, not a subject and not a puppet or object.

4. Trust (faith, belief). The actualizer has a deep trust in himself and others to relate to and cope with life in the here and now.

1. From *Man, the Manipulator*, by Everett Shostrom (Nashville, Tenn.: Abingdon, 1967). Copyright ©1967 by Abingdon Press. Reprinted by permission of the publisher.

Any techniques you adopt or devise to help your students learn self-discipline—and no system can include the variety and complexity of situations you encounter—are effective in most cases if applied with honesty, awareness, openness, and trust. To provide conditions for development of such attributes in students, you are urged to establish a democratic classroom.

THE DEMOCRATIC CLASSROOM

By inviting your students to help you establish a set of rules for keeping an orderly and productive classroom, you earn their confidence in you and simultaneously gain a substantial measure of their support in maintaining consistent discipline.

Obviously, a student is less likely to consider you unfair if the rule he has just broken is one he helped to make and the consequence he must bear is one he had a voice in determining. You find students more willing to follow rules and to assume their associated consequences when the rules belong to them. This not only makes it easier for a teacher to administer discipline fairly, it is an important step in teaching students to assume responsibility for their own actions. When children know what is expected of them and can foresee the results of a given behavior, consistency is more easily preserved; more important, the youngsters realize they are a significant part of the disciplinary process.

RULES FOR STUDENTS

Hold class rap sessions or business meetings early in the school year to decide on rules for behavior in the room, halls, lunchroom, and playground and to make lists of rules plus the consequences for offending them. The children in your class know themselves better than anyone else knows them. They are aware of behaviors that have caused them to be placed in a special classroom. You'll discover that some of the students whose behavior is least acceptable seem to be most knowledgeable on what is acceptable—and that these very children tend to favor more stringent rules as well as stiffer penalties than you might wish to employ.

Make it clear that you're open to suggestions for rules covering classroom and other school conduct. When you write suggestions on the chalkboard, be sure to state them positively. (Instead of, "No running in or bumping in the hall," write, "Walk in the hall and stay clear of others.") It's a good idea at this time to talk about why we have rules and the reason for each rule (safety; consideration of others).

After the rules are written, ask the class to help you list them in order of importance. Talk about why rule number one should carry greater weight than rule number ten. Follow up with a list of consequences for breaking each rule, assigning more severe consequences to more important rules. (For example, failure to control body and voice while angry would be a more serious offense than failure to remain quiet while others are talking.)

Usually, it is necessary to help students decide on less serious consequences than those they suggest; and you can counter advice favoring physical punishment with remarks such as, "Can't we think of something more suitable?" Consequences, usually based on deprivation, can include loss of snacks, of recess, of free time at the activity center, or of other rewards and privileges. (A full discussion of consequences is presented in chapter 13.) When the lists are copied on poster paper and placed conspicuously at the front of the room, the students have a set of well-understood behavioral guidelines, along with specifically derived positive and negative consequences. Because of differences in class composition, lists vary from year to year. They should be altered and added to as needs arise, particularly soon after a new student is admitted.

Before calling the first rap session, set forth a few basic rules on conduct of a business meeting to ensure an orderly discussion—rather than chance chaos at the very beginning of your project to establish order.

RULES FOR TEACHER

Students never fail to show enthusiasm for establishing their own codes of conduct. When called upon to help make a set of rules for their teacher's behavior, they react with disbelief and excitement. With a minimum of encouragement, students pour forth complaints describing teachers who yell, who are mean, who won't give help when asked for, who give work that's too hard, and who are grouchy all the time. After writing these things down, you can reword them positively for your own set of rules, using such phrases as "speak in a quiet voice," "show kindness," and so forth. Almost inevitably, before the discussion is over, some child will remark, "A teacher should be nice and also strict"; this can be restated as "fair, yet firm."

Stating your own guidelines constitutes a pledge of your sincere intentions, demonstrates your openness, and reinforces the students' commitment to their behavior standards.

CONSISTENCY

Total consistency in behavior is an ideal nobody can reach. Should you inadvertently betray the fact that you're human by losing your patience and yelling in front of the class, admit you have broken a rule and lead a discussion on how you should have handled the situation. Showing the ability to admit error provides modeling on the real-life level, which is infinitely more effective than modeling through role playing (which is treated at the end of this chapter).

However, consistency on your part is of prime importance. If a child breaks a rule that prescribes his waiting to be called on before speaking and you are too preoccupied to deliver the assigned consequence, the rule becomes worthless. If there is a rule against nagging for permission and you allow yourself to be worn down by a nagging student to the point that you exclaim "Oh, go ahead!" there is no point in leaving that rule posted.

Occasionally a student complains that you are refusing to give help when it is needed. If you are positive the student can do the work himself, the burden of proof is on you. Accurate judgment will depend on knowledge of the student's abilities as demonstrated in previous performance, whether or not he has been absent, and other circumstances. It is wise never to refuse help outright, but to limit the amount of attention you give a demanding child. When you see a student using devious means to get your help on an assignment he considers difficult and wishes to avoid, find the most direct method you can to deal with the problem without withholding all help. One approach is to place a limited number of chips or counters on the child's desk, telling him, "Each one of these stands for five minutes free time if you keep it, but I'll take one back for each question you ask. When they're gone, no more questions and no free time—so you must decide when you really need help." After once going through all his counters within the first two or three minutes, the child becomes more selective in his questions. Eventually, he'll do his utmost to complete assignments alone—not perfectly, perhaps, but perfection is not the object of this exercise.

Consistency in using a positive approach serves to win students' cooperation in many situations where negative answers would arouse hostilities due to frustration. You encounter many circumstances in which a youngster insists on being allowed to do something that would be disruptive or irrelevant at the moment; your first impulse is to answer no. Since intolerance for the word *no* is even stronger in emotionally impaired children than in normal ones, give a little thought to developing the habit of saying no by saying yes. You can do this simply by replying, "Yes, you can do what you ask as soon as this class is over"; or, "Of course you may tell us about that—after you finish your math." In this way, you deny a request, but do so positively. The child feels less thwarted and perceives more incentive to be patient and/or complete required work.

Other no answers that can be delivered through positive responses are, "Helen, we'll enjoy looking at those Japanese prints during social studies," and (while taking possession of a toy brought to school), "Oh, Ozzie, won't you have fun with this race car during free time?"

PRINCIPLE OF
CONTROLLED
FREEDOM

The democratic classroom fosters self-discipline through a principle of controlled freedom. Controlled freedom describes a situation with a tight, well-defined structure within which free choices are offered. Students feel responsible to the structure because they have contributed to setting up rules and consequences. They can make choices within the structure (such as deciding what subject they wish to take up first in the morning) but never a choice that would weaken the structure (such as to shirk a subject completely). Also, although he has a free choice between a number of free-time activities, no child can engage in free-time activity whenever he desires; and during free time he must stick with the activity he has chosen.

When everyone knows in advance what consequence follows refusal to stay within the structure, coercion and nagging about completion of assignments becomes unnecessary. If your reward for getting work done before recess is a midmorning snack after recess, a dawdling child is fully aware that unless his work is completed he will lose his snack. No word from you is needed. Should the child go to recess without completing the assignment, you simply withhold his reward. If he chooses to continue the behavior, he continues to forfeit snacks of his own free will. Finally he will realize that by leaving assignments unfinished he is depriving only himself, both gradewise and in loss of the rewards.

MODELING AND
ROLE-PLAYING

A valuable supplement to check sheet evaluations of behavior and class rap sessions on rules of conduct is the introduction of role playing for demonstration of appropriate reactions to typical conflict situations. Used as a game, modeling provides enjoyment while delivering an impact not contained in lists of right and wrong ways to behave. It requires teachers to be able to engage in exaggerated play acting and to share laughter with a class.

Initiated without warning, the modeling of some drastically inappropriate reaction to an interpersonal conflict is sure to shock your students to rapt attention. An immediate replay of the scene, this time demonstrating socially acceptable reactions, makes the class aware of what's happening and prepares them to join in the role playing.

Prearrange a time for your aide to bump into you ''accidentally'' while you are writing at the chalkboard or leading class discussion. Instantly, pretend to fly into a rage because you were bumped. Draw your arms back in a fighting pose or even strike at the aide, shouting, ''Can't you look where you're going?'' Ignore the aide's attempts to placate you, and keep up the act until the students begin to realize it is an act. Then replay the situation, this time using courtesy and an understanding attitude toward the ''accident.''

Students are eager to take part in role playing, and there is no end to the variety of situations that can be dramatized. Students can act out lunchroom and school bus experiences, their own interrelationships, and rules they have instigated. Role playing and behavior modeling provide moralizing without being moralistic. They teach socially acceptable values by furnishing actual practice in behaviors that some children might never learn any other way, simply because *doing* a thing helps them become more comfortable with newly acquired problem-solving techniques.

Children who are habitually disruptive may often be surprisingly self-conscious when asked to play a disruptive role (they may even have to be urged on). These children tend also to be the best actors when modeling appropriate behaviors, thus creating a chance for you and the class to applaud them.

Children can be taught to ignore all disruptions by individual students (for example, to continue classroom routine while a tantrum is going on) through modeling. Students quickly comprehend your reasons for not attending inappropriate behavior and learn to cooperate in the practice by unanimously ignoring a disruptive student (placing him ''on extinction''). This cooperation is especially effective on rare occasions when one student has deliberately broken a major class rule, because being placed on extinction by everyone in the room is the worst punishment that can be dealt to a young offender.

Role playing provides useful rehearsal for actual experiences in practicing self-discipline and avoids didactic verbalization on the subject. Nevertheless, your paramount aim will be to help your students make real use of self-discipline in their daily lives.

SELF-DISCIPLINE FOR TEACHER

Since each student in your classroom has a uniquely individual background of experiences, teaching self-discipline requires a variety of approaches. Chapters to come present general descriptions of various behavior disorders you must be prepared to encounter in the classroom. As you peruse those chapters, bear in mind the following points:

1. Emotional impairment differs from normal according to the relative intensities and frequencies of unacceptable behaviors and according to their setting and timing. All behaviors that characterize emotionally impaired children are found in normal children; and this statement can be reversed. Your students are neither mindless beings ruled by emotions nor automatons who can be expected to respond predictably to given stimuli. Rather, they are a group of youngsters who, to function acceptably in ordinary classrooms, must learn to use normal frequencies, intensities, and settings for certain behaviors. (For example, laughter is a behavior that could be considered appropriate or inappropriate, depending on its frequency, intensity, place, and time.)

2. Diagnostic nomenclature should be approached with reservation. Each child's diagnosis alerts you to types of behaviors to anticipate, but beware of basing your attitude toward any child on his diagnostic profile. You cannot pre-suppose that a given behavior will show itself in your class, because your class provides a different environment than students have know previously. Test results on a youngster are sometimes several months old by the time he reaches a special classroom; and a test lasting one to three hours is at best only a representative sampling of a child's total makeup. Therefore, in your one-to-one relationship with a student,

you may never observe behaviors that were recorded on his profile, and you may notice others that were previously overlooked. Be prepared—as you would in any classroom—for unexpected actions and reactions; then proceed to guide students into school routines that relegate disruptions to a minor role.

3. Never accept unreservedly a diagnostic conclusion that assumes limits on a child's growth potential. Test batteries tell only where a student is as a result of his prior learning experiences. New experiences (individualized instruction, provision of incentives for growth both academically and emotionally, and positive parent involvement when possible) can open up a whole new world to a youngster. It is impossible to predict the effects of new environmental factors on a child's capacities for growth.

4. The teacher is the source of stabilization in any classroom. When you have established rules that are known to everyone, students look to you for strong leadership in their enforcement. There is no way to become completely forearmed against every possible development except through absolute confidence in your own judgment, which is communicated to aides and students by the unhurried objectivity with which you meet each problem as it arises. To dispel any apprehensions you may have about coping with some of the behaviors described in your course work, you must recognize that no single class for emotionally impaired children includes students who exhibit more than a fraction of the listed behaviors. As a matter of fact, it is doubtful that you'll ever encounter all the types of behavior that are discussed in this book. Specific individual behavior eludes precise description.

5. The teacher must have interests and activities not related to school interests and activities. For protection of your own mental health, it is imperative that you be involved in hobbies or an avocation that helps you maintain a healthy perspective during your free hours away from school. Although your acceptance and understanding are vital to your students, your becoming immersed in their problems is detrimental to their growth as well as to yours. Avoid brooding over your class or over individual students and don't worry about mistakes; do your best each day, learn from each experience, but keep your own life separate. Overconcern for students, in addition to threatening vital disciplinary consistency, can result in a teacher's becoming reluctant to face each decision to let a child go after he or she has proved ready to move on to another classroom.

5

AGGRESSIVE BEHAVIORS

I've always been a cutup. I think it helps people get through a lot. It's a defense. A lot of comedy comes from bad things, from a lot of pain.

Also, you can just be naturally funny. I think I have it somewhere in my bones that I see things funny. The best moment I can remember in junior high school, my crowning moment, came after an assembly. The principal dismissed the assembly by homerooms . . . and he called out one homeroom after another. . . . When he got to [our homeroom] he started dismissing us by rows, and then our row was left, and he dismissed us by students, and I was the only one left . . . with the rest of the school on the periphery, and the principal boomed into the microphone, ''Lewis, you're the troublemaker of this junior high school!''

That was it. It was like playing the Copa. I took bows. That was the reinforcement I was looking for. So I was a clown.[1]

RICHARD LEWIS, comedian; quoted by Edward Zuckerman in
Harper's Weekly.

1. Edward Zuckerman, *Harper's Weekly*, 27 June 1975.

Aggressiveness is not only normal in most children but a necessary trait for successful survival. However, children who consistently lose control of their aggressiveness, to a point that it is detrimental to themselves and/or harmful to those around them, need guidance in learning to use the trait in ways that will benefit them and be socially acceptable. Class rap sessions, role playing and student-teacher conferences promote conscious recognition of advantages to be gained by controlling aggressive behaviors, but youngsters with severe impairments in this area must have day-to-day help in meeting difficult situations as they arise.

This chapter discusses overt aggressiveness as it is displayed in clowning, teasing and bullying, tattling and nagging, general hostility, and temper tantrums.

CLOWNING   Excessive clowning and showing off to get attention can be termed aggressive behaviors because of their tendency to disrupt classroom activities. Far from being a characteristic that should be extinguished, the ability to arouse laughter is an admirable quality, which, channeled appropriately, is beneficial to a world that needs all the laughs it can get.

Exhibitionism, although normal in very young children, is a sign of immaturity in youngsters over six years of age. It is normal at any age to enjoy being considered clever; but the individual who strives to be the butt of every joke, who wants to be laughed at by others but cannot share in all kinds of humor, is likely to be compensating for emotional impairment.

Occasionally, you encounter a student who grasps every chance to gain attention through antics such as imitating an ape, jumping off tables while shouting, "Look at me—I'm Superman!" or deliberately stumbling and falling to make his classmates laugh. Often this type of child shows above-average intelligence, a well-developed sense of humor, and such excellent timing that he invariably succeeds in winning appreciative giggles from his peers—and in making you struggle to keep a straight face. But keep a straight face you must; for such a child needs to learn discrimination between circumstances in which his buffoonery is appropriate and those in which it is not. Any kind of attention he receives while clowning not only encourages him to disrupt the class but also serves to strengthen his mask.

Show neither approval nor disapproval, then, to clowning behavior that disrupts the class. Explain to your students that everyone will have a chance to share jokes and fun at break time or when the day's work has been completed; then praise them for attending to their lessons whenever such disruptions occur. At specifically designated times each day, give the young clown and other students opportunities to tell (or write) funny stories, either true or fictional, with emphasis on the difference between reality and imagination. Involve the class in humorous dramatizations in which the clown plays leading parts. Take every possible opportunity to help such a child gain attention through behaviors that are acceptable in a classroom situation. As he begins to feel he can gain approval without resorting to pretense, his facade grows less rigid and he becomes more capable of confronting his emotional problems—without having his facility for wit and exuberance destroyed.

TEASING AND BULLYING

The youngster who seems to take delight in harrassing another child until the victim is driven to react emotionally appears callous and cruel. The normal adult instinctively springs to the defense of the victim, then tries to instill gentleness and peace in the bully through punishment, lecturing, or both. Unfortunately, this method is usually fruitless because it reinforces the behaviors of both culprit and victim.

The first focus of therapy is the victim, whose fear and tendency to lose control invite bullying. The more promptly and emotionally such a child reacts to harrassment, the more he stimulates his tormenter; and the sympathetic attention he receives from others serves to reinforce the entire process.

It should not be necessary to specify that a bully caught in the act of doing physical harm must be restrained, but any attempts to discuss the matter rationally with him immediately after the occurrence would be a waste of breath. Without comment on what he has done, automatically dispense whatever punishment the class rules have stipulated for the offense. When you confer with him on his check sheet evaluations at the end of the day, talk about the mark he is getting and the behavior that prompted it without going into details of what happened or moralizing to him.

Meanwhile, the victim should be helped to learn that ignoring advances made by an aggressor discourages the aggressor. In private conversations, make it clear to him that nobody has the power to hurt him unless he allows it to happen. With your support, he can gain enough confidence in himself to maintain indifference to taunts or even blows, which eventually effects an alteration in his relationship with the other child.

George, who frequently ran to his teacher complaining that an older boy from another room had bullied him on the playground, was told to ignore all harrassment and show active interest in playground games. With the teacher's daily support, he learned gradually to follow this advice, but the aggressor continued his attempts to force George to lose self-control. The teacher happened to be watching through a window on the day this struggle reached its climax, and witnessed the following.

When George emerged from the building, the other boy, who was waiting for him, began to taunt and threaten him. George withstood four attempts the boy made to get his attention; then the boy jumped on his back. In a purely reflex action, George swung around and drove his fist squarely into the other boy's mouth. Stunned, the boy released his grip and George immediately returned to his room to report the incident.

Admitting having observed his four attempts to avoid physical confrontation, the teacher praised George for doing his best and added, "I think you handled it without losing your cool."

George was then taken to the principal, to whom he reported the matter with corroboration from the teacher—a step the teacher considered necessary to avoid repercussions, since the other boy was not a classmate of George's.

The older boy's harrassments ceased abruptly and from that day on he managed to give George a wide berth on the playground.

While no teacher should advocate the use of violence, in this case the teacher was obliged to approve George's method of self-defense because he had made a sincere effort to avoid physical confrontation.

When both bully and victim are members of your class, the likelihood of altering their interrelationship in a positive way increases. By sharing rap sessions and role playing that examine and demonstrate various responses to all kinds of behaviors, they begin to recognize their own hang-ups and also to learn some insight into the effectiveness of self-discipline.

In the following study, quoted in part, a student was coached to make definite prearranged responses to another student's teasing behavior.

The target behavior in this project was "name-calling" on the part of an eleven-year-old boy in the authors' classroom. The name-calling consisted of the boy's calling another eleven-year-old boy "Keify." This resulted in extremely negative verbal responses on the part of the second boy. After observing this interaction for several days, the authors decided to try to eliminate this name-calling in the first boy (S) by using the second boy as the experimenter (E).

The study was divided into two phases. The first, or baseline, phase lasted seven days. During this time period, each time S would call E "Keify," E was to respond by saying such things as "Cut that out," "Quit it," and "Don't call me that," using an angry tone of voice. After the baseline data had stabilized, the second phase was started. During the experimental phase, each time S addressed E without using "Keify," E would respond by saying, "Thank you for not calling me Keify," or, "I'm glad you didn't call me Keify," and E would continue to interact with S. Each time, however, that S called E "Keify" during this phase, E would completely ignore S and walk away, thereby terminating any interaction between the two for a period of time not specified. By the fourth day of the second phase, the name-calling had dropped to zero.[2]

While such deliberately controlled manipulation is not advisable in most circumstances and it should not be used outside a formal study, encouraging children to ignore harrassment, as a general technique combined with other classroom procedures can help the aggressor become conscious of his habit in practice as well as in theory.

Whereas the clown attempts to shield underlying emotional turmoil by making himself an object of ridicule, the tease or bully attempts the same thing by centering ridicule on others. Socially, the latter behavior is both less acceptable and more difficult to deal with; however, the approaches that have been discussed can yield good results. In addition, at the beginning the teacher should make sure to bestow generous approval, when it is warranted, of even the most minor successes achieved by such children in any area of endeavor. As the children gain self-acceptance and trust, their need to inflict pain diminishes.

TATTLING

The child who persistently demands a teacher's attention by tattling, nagging, or whining learns to reduce such behavior only when it receives no attention whatever from the teacher. You can tell a tattler to mind his own business and let others take care of their own problems a thousand times without helping him to learn to distinguish between incidents that are trivial and those serious enough to be reported. If you seek out the child who has been told on for reprimand or punishment, you reinforce the tattler.

Assume that any event unwitnessed by yourself or another supervising adult lacks sufficient importance to warrant investigation (unless brought to your attention by a child who does not habitually tattle). Should the tattler claim to be the victim of an injustice, advise him as you would a victim of actual harrassment: tell him to ignore it.

2. Doris Mosier and J.J. Vaal, Jr., "The Manipulation of One Child's Behavior by Another Child in a School Adjustment Classroom," *School Application of Learning Theory*, Kalamazoo Valley Intermediate School District, Kalamazoo, Mich., vol 11, no. 2 (April 1970).

Diane, a second grader, bombarded her teacher with constant tattling, which became disruptive to the entire school routine. Finally the teacher consulted a colleague, supervisor of a class for emotionally impaired children, who agreed to assist in studying the problem.

The teacher was advised first to set up a baseline by keeping a record of the frequency of Diane's tattling over a two-day period, during which the teacher would continue to respond as usual. Frequencies recorded were sixteen and eighteen, respectively.

Following establishment of the baseline, the teacher was instructed to ignore all tattling behavior from Diane but to give her generous attention and praise for acceptable behaviors. Eye contact during tattling was to be withheld by the teacher.

Frequency of the behavior increased sharply at first, but, after five days of consistently ignoring Diane's tattling, the teacher reported the occurrence had dropped to twice in one day. Following the weekend, frequency rose temporarily then decreased by the end of the second week to zero.

Some time later, Diane's teacher overheard her saying to another child, "It won't do any good to tell teacher 'cause she won't listen." In addition, Diane's mother (who had been unaware of the teacher's project) reported that the child had decreased her frequency of tattling on her brothers and sisters at home.

NAGGING

Students who badger a teacher with requests for permission to do intrusive things are in the same category as the tattler and in most cases can be helped to eliminate their habits by the same methods. Sometimes the technique of saying no while saying yes will placate such a child, but when nagging is persistent and accompanied by whining the most effective method is to ignore the behavior.

Once started on the procedure, you cannot allow yourself to be worn down by a persistent nagger, whose determination to command your attention will intensify at the beginning to the point that he uses drastic action in trying to enforce his will. If you maintain consistency, however, his efforts dwindle and the approval you show him at other times aids him in adjusting to a less aggressive role.

HOSTILITY

Overt hostility manifests itself in elementary school children less often in the form of physical violence than in threatening language and gestures. Youngsters described as hostile appear to seethe with anger at their total environment. One such child may be a genuinely frustrated individual whose home relationships are a constant disappointment and whose academic performance, because of his emotional turmoil, lags far behind his intellectual potential. Another may come from a family that is always on the defensive, where everyone "talks tough" and uses menacing behavior as a matter of course. In either case, role playing, student-teacher conferences, and conscious attention to target behaviors are helpful in teaching the child to practice self-discipline.

As an authority figure, you are a prime object of distrust; for this reason, you may have to prove your sincerity and reliability many times before the student gains confidence in you. It must be emphasized that this cannot be accomplished through superficial words or by granting unearned privileges; on the other hand, when you are certain that a child is making a supreme effort to control his behavior, a timely special award might tend to be more effective than generous verbal approval. The example that follows illustrates this view.

When ten-year-old Lloyd entered a class for emotionally impaired children he bristled with antagonism, all of it vented in verbal expressions such as, "Say that again and you'll get these scissors in your ear." The target behavior established with the help of his teacher was stated in the words, "I will be kind to everyone today." A point system was set up by which the child received a minus for each hostile comment and a plus for an acceptable one. The teacher's reinforcement consisted of praise for every appropriate response the student made to her or to a classmate—which were so few in comparison to the number of hostile ones that a month later, when Lloyd began to show progress, he had accumulated so many negative points that it looked impossible for him ever to get on the plus side of the record. The teacher continued to encourage him but said nothing more until Lloyd had succeeded in getting through a full day without receiving a minus point. At the end of that day, on reviewing his check sheets with him, the teacher said, "I have been noticing how hard you're trying and I feel you deserve a special award." She took the previous check sheets away, informing him, "You're getting a brand new start." Grinning up at the teacher, the child said, "Ya know, you're an all right guy!" and from that time on his hostile behavior remained at low frequency, finally disappearing altogether. On a later occasion when the teacher had reason to praise him for something, Lloyd's rejoinder was, "You know why—look what you did for me."

TEMPER TANTRUMS   The better you know a child who is prone to temper paroxysm, the greater are your chances of preventing a tantrum by intervening in a situation that you know might lead to one. While you are getting acquainted with the child, it is wise to be ready to face episodes involving violent anger in the classroom.

It is totally ineffective to try to reason with a youngster while he is engaging in tantrum behavior; as a matter of fact, any attention at all might only increase the probability of prolonging the tantrum and/or encouraging its repetition in the future. Attempts at reassurance, offering the child a drink of water to divert his attention, or commanding him to overcome his emotion will tend to make the behavior more severe. A child in tantrum should be left alone to work out his anger.

Naturally, you cannot remain utterly indifferent to someone in the throes of uncontrollable turmoil. Lead the child gently but steadfastly to an area that gives him the most possible privacy, then return to the business of the class. If you remain calm, the class will follow your example. After the student has regained control of himself, you can welcome him back to the class with words such as, "We're glad you feel better and I think you did a good job of getting yourself together *all by yourself.*" This can be done in front of the class or privately, depending on the student's individual needs and stage of progress. Then, proceed as if nothing had happened.

At a later time, when the child has completely recovered and when you're free to do so, find time to talk quietly to the child about what happened, what precipitated it, and what he could have done to vent his anger in a more meaningful way. Never give a child the idea that you think it wrong to feel angry or hurt, but help him find effective methods for dealing with his emotions by verbalizing them rationally and by consciously deciding not to react violently. You can tell him that talking about feeling angry and explaining his reasons can help other people understand his point of view, so that differences can be aired and reasonable compromises can be made.

During class rap sessions, encourage discussion on how people's feelings get hurt and on the fact that everyone gets angry at times. Talk about ways to control emotion, and how an individual can stave off hurt by refusing to allow name-calling or other offenses to bother him. When children understand that it is actually within their own power to decide whether to express anger, they often make rapid progress toward self-discipline.

To demonstrate the point, you can improvise role playing in which various comments and gestures arouse different reactions, according to the way they are interpreted. Expressions such as, "You're crazy!" or, "That's really cool!"—or gestures such as a slap on the back—can be used to show that a person's level of security or self-confidence can determine how he receives them. Children can be helped to understand that their interpretations of others' behavior can sometimes be more a function of their own thoughts and feelings than a function of what the other person intended to express. In addition, this kind of role playing helps youngsters comprehend that another individual's outright aggression may stem from a generalized basic insecurity, so it should not be taken personally. Above all, the fact that any person can *choose* how he responds to hostility and aggression is valuable knowledge to a child who is learning to control his own behavior.

6
PASSIVE BEHAVIORS

I hardly played any games; I made no friends . . . I cried in bed at night . . . I gradually became a nervous wreck, for whom trifling difficulties assumed the proportions of acute misery. . . .

Who realizes that for some boys at school an undeserved imposition may cause as much mental anguish as the death of a friend will later on? Who really appreciates that something quite trivial may cause in certain immature minds an emotional upset which may in a very short time inflict incurable damage?

I told no one and said nothing about it. My natural sensitiveness increased till it became pathological and my mind was an open wound. The slightest touch produced twinges of pain and agonizing repercussions which did me permanent harm. Happy indeed are those to whom nature has given a thick skin and the armor of stoicism!

GUY DE MAUPASSANT, *Looking Back*

Passive behaviors are characterized by secretiveness and preference for solitude. Such behaviors are likely to make a child appear fearful of interpersonal relationships, or aloof and disdainful toward others, or unresponsive to the point of seeming impervious to his surroundings. Behaviors to be discussed under this heading are withdrawal, autism, masturbation, clumsiness, and stuttering.

Children who exhibit withdrawn behavior tend to avoid associating with others. Typical withdrawn individuals shy away from eye contact, indicate embarrassment and awkwardness when asked to read aloud or recite, and shrink back from group activities. It's essential to keep at a low key and a cautiously slow rate any efforts at helping a withdrawn child develop normal aggressiveness. Once the student begins to show trust in the classroom environment, the rate of encouragement can be accelerated; however, remain alert to any situation in which the child has previously reacted as if he felt threatened.

In her regular third-grade classroom, Margie incessantly hid her face behind her hands. She refused to recite and was unresponsive to her teacher's efforts to include her in class activities. She kept to herself on the playground. The child would work alone at her desk, making precise handwritten copies of printed materials but showing aversion to trying anything new. Whenever any original or creative writing was assigned her she wrote in short, stilted sentences that contained no imagination.

Placed in a special classroom where enrollment was limited and the atmosphere noncompetitive, Margie began to change rapidly. The teacher encouraged another girl in the room (who was quiet, but not withdrawn) to do art projects with her. Both youngsters became absorbed in working with watercolors; to do away with exact copying and rigidity of form, the teacher had them paint on paper that had been wet so that colors would run and blur together. Margie was reinforced only moderately at first, since enthusiastic praise seemed to embarrass her. Gradually she exhibited tolerance for attention and finally began to indicate that she enjoyed it. When the teacher saw her smile for the first time, after noting the flicker of a smile on the child's face, the teacher remarked, "You're pretty when you smile."

A supervising adult from the special classroom accompanied Margie to the playground daily at first, for the purpose of slowly drawing the child into group play. As her friendship with the other girl developed, Margie found the playground less intimidating, showing this by beginning to jump rope and participate in other games.

Although this student never became boisterous or impulsive, she did begin to laugh aloud, to speak out before the class and to try new things without hesitation. She returned to her previous school district within a few months with the ability to function normally as well as to make friends with peers who had shunned her in the past.

Not all withdrawn behavior can be modified in as brief a span of time or as effectively as it was in the case of Margie. The most important part of therapy in all similar cases, however, is casualness and moderation in your original advances to the child, followed by steady but slow-paced increases in attention as the child manifests tolerance for it.

AUTISM

The word *autism* has become a catchall too often applied to young children whose behaviors indicate varying degrees of withdrawal. Not much is understood about true autism, which is withdrawal behavior so severe that it results in cutting off practically all contact with the social environment.

True autism is so rare that it is unlikely you will ever encounter it in the classroom, even though you may be expected to work with some children so withdrawn that they neither speak nor appear to hear what is said to them. When you encounter a student who has been diagnosed autistic, your first action should be to ascertain whether all possibilities of physiological and neurological causes have been explored. Being an aspect of the psychosis known as schizophrenia, the condition may in some instances be medically treatable, not to effect a cure so much as to facilitate social and academic therapy. Along with checking on other possible physical causes, insist on a complete hearing examination (unless one has been done recently). Without auditory stimulation, a young child is likely to appear—or perhaps even learn to appear—autistic, particularly if he has encountered painful social experiences.

This excerpt from Josh Greenfeld's book *A Child Called Noah* describes one parent's frustrations concerning diagnosis of a youngster whose symptoms indicated autism.

What's the matter with Noah? For the longest time it seemed to depend upon what diagnosis we were willing to shop around for. We'd been told he was mentally retarded; emotionally disturbed; autistic; schizophrenic; possibly brain-damaged; or he was suffering from a Chinese-box combination of these conditions. But we finally discovered that the diagnosis didn't seem to matter; it was all so sadly academic. The medical profession was merely playing Aristotelian nomenclature and classification games at our expense. For though we live in one of the richest states in the nation, there was no single viable treatment immediately available for Noah, no matter what category he could eventually be assigned to. . . .

And not the least victims of this common but rarely foreseen malady will be the child's parents and family. They may delight at first in the tranquil docility or uncommon beauty of their child. For schizophrenic children are very often—and autistic children are invariably—beautiful, as if their untouchable imperviousness to the usual course of human events keeps them so. Then, however, there will be months and years of anguish, roller-coaster cycles of elation and depression as the parents try to deny the evidence before their eyes that their child is less than ordinary or normal, is indeed "exceptional," to use one of the medical euphemisms. In addition, parents will find themselves getting little in the way of help and much in the way of confusion from the medical profession. Most neurologists, they will discover, would rather describe than prescribe; most psychiatrists are more apt to make the parents feel guilty than to suggest a program to help the child. After a while the local pediatrician himself may begin to regard both child and parents as troublemakers and deviants, out to disrupt his rounds of runny noses and infected ears.[1]

When a diagnostician concludes that a given child cannot be induced to react to any stimulus, when the child seems to be turned inward and apparently oblivious to everything about him, he may be pronounced beyond diagnosis or he may be designated autistic. Despite such discouraging findings, a skillful therapist can often lead such a child into contact with his world. In her work with neurologically impaired children, Dr. Else Haeussermann discovered that, when left in isolation with test materials while the examiner was absent from view, some apparently autistic youngsters would independently complete test items or at least show curiosity concerning test materials.[2] This suggests that certain ex-

1. Josh Greenfeld, *A Child Called Noah* (New York: Warner Paperbacks, 1973), pp. 14–15. Copyright © 1970, 1971, 1972 by Josh Greenfeld. Reprinted by permission of Holt, Rinehart and Winston, Publishers.

2. Else Haeussermann, *Developmental Potential of Preschool Children* (New York: Grune and Stratton, 1958), chap. 7.

tremely withdrawn children employ pretense as a part of an overall facade that is used to exclude all intrusions on their self-imposed retreat from socially imposed stimuli.

Here is a case history that illustrates both the mysteriousness of autism and the importance of sensitivity on the part of a therapist attempting to deal with it.

Ten-year-old Vernon was placed in a special classroom with a diagnosis of autism and borderline mental impairment. His mother reported that the boy, first of four siblings, had been the only one of her children who never demanded attention as an infant, leading her to regard him as "a good baby." She said Vernon had from the start accepted care passively but had never cried for food, never protested when put to bed, and when rocked or given undue attention he had stiffened in resistance. By the time he came to the room for emotionally impaired children, Vernon's self-isolation both at home and at school had led his parents to believe his condition was hopeless.

In the new room, Vernon ignored the teacher's suggestion that he be seated. He lay on the floor in a supine position, making occasional meaningless sounds and body movements and ignoring his surroundings—except that, on being approached, he would make pushing-away gestures. During recess period, he moved to sit near the door, still apparently oblivious to the actions of others; however, he did respond to lunch call and to the teacher's instructions to the class at going-home time.

The teacher instructed his classmates to ignore Vernon. He continued to lie on the floor daily, with the teacher pretending he was not there, and everyone casually stepping around him. After about a week had passed, Vernon surprised the teacher by abruptly telling her how many bulbs in the hall lights had burned out. The teacher thanked him for the information but registered no indication that his talking was considered unusual. Two days later, the boy again broke into speech to announce the number of holes in the room's acoustic ceiling. This time he received praise from the teacher and was asked how he had counted them. He explained that he had counted the holes along sides of a single square of acoustical material, multiplied to get the number in one square, then had counted squares in the entire ceiling by the same method and made a final multiplication to arrive at the total.

Up until the day he counted the holes in the ceiling, Vernon had made no response to the teacher's daily morning greeting, and his announcement concerning the burned-out light bulbs had been his only previous words to anyone. Commenting on his feat in multiplication, the teacher said, "Vernon, that was a remarkable accomplishment and you have earned the right to sit at your desk." To the teacher's (completely unexpressed) amazement, the boy rose and took his seat.

The teacher then casually handed Vernon a pencil and some paper with the words, "I see you like to do really hard problems." The child drew away from direct contact without reply, but he allowed the materials to be placed on his desk, so the teacher opened a fifth-grade math book to multiplication problems using three-digit multipliers and placed it with the pencil and paper, adding in a matter-of-fact voice, "When you have worked the first problem, raise your hand." Vernon complied with the instructions.

The teacher followed through by remarking, "You probably couldn't do the whole page," to which the boy reacted by casting a look of contempt in the direction of the teacher while muttering, "Yuk!" Not knowing how to interpret this, the teacher walked away and proceeded to pay Vernon no further attention until he raised his hand after completing all the problems. The teacher praised his accomplishment sincerely and handed him some plastic chips, which he grasped eagerly. Apparently he had been observing the use of token economy in the room and was aware of the value of his chips, because he counted them as if prizing them highly.

The first time Vernon was given a reading book he threw it at the teacher. A couple of days were allowed to pass before the book was offered again by being placed on the child's desk. He ignored it, taking out his math book. The teacher said, "Would you like to do some more math? When you have read a story to yourself, you will have earned the privilege to do more math."

Vernon again betrayed his understanding of classroom procedures, observed while on the floor and pretending to be detached from it all, when he set about reading—or making a pretext of reading—the teacher was unable to discern which. Later he raised his hand and at a nod from the teacher, took up his math. In this manner he gradually joined the class.

During free-time periods the teacher frequently noticed Vernon examining extension cords and electrical outlets in the room. Recalling that his first communication had been about light bulbs, the teacher decided to appeal to the boy's interest in electricity. A simple kit containing a dry cell battery with wires that would hook up to activate a bell, a light, or a clicking metronome was introduced to the class during science period, eliciting Vernon's first expression of enthusiasm. He actually jumped from his seat and tried to take possession of the experiment. He was told he could earn time to work with it by staying in his seat (he was still returning to the horizontal position occasionally) and by doing his assignments. It was then explained to Vernon and the class that working with the kit was to be his exclusive privilege; other students would be expected to work for other privileges.

Requirements made of Vernon were now stiffened a little more each day. He was given increasingly difficult math and reading assignments and asked questions demanding greater comprehension, which had to be answered before he could work with the kit. After completing a task he was allowed a specific length of time with the kit, with another task being required before he could return to it. First he assembled the kit, then he brought extra wire from home and arranged it to activate the bell, light, and metronome simultaneously. One day he volunteered to fix a cord in the room that was frayed and broken and was praised for fixing it.

Next, a kit for building an ohm-meter was brought in, and necessary tools were provided by Vernon's father. A table was installed in a corner for this project and the boy put up a sign that said, "Repair Shop."

With this, requirements for privileges were shifted to social skills. Vernon was expected to say "Good morning" and to respond to his classmates instead of making gestures of rejection.

By the end of the school year, Vernon had gained a schoolwide reputation for his skill with electrical materials, having fixed appliances for several teachers and also having repaired several sets of old headphones the teacher had rescued from the trash. On one occasion, after drawing applause from the entire student body for mending an extension cord that was needed for the public address system in a musical assembly program, the immoderate attention nearly overwhelmed him, but with his teacher's support, he managed to avoid panic. In his workshop at school, he built his own AM-FM radio during free time earned by completing assignments.

During summer vacation, Vernon joined a 4-H electrical club, winning first prize with his project. On phasing him into a regular classroom that fall, the teacher commented, "Although not the most sociable child in the world, Vernon no longer turns away from others; in fact, his groping for interaction has caused him to become somewhat of a tease."

It should be emphasized that the results reported in Vernon's case could not have been foreseen and that therapy was shaped, as all behavior therapy should be, around the student's reactions on a day-to-day basis. It cannot be assumed that all children who have been diagnosed "autistic" will respond to similar treatment; however, bear in mind that, since both frequency and intensity of attention tend to increase the severity of withdrawal symptoms, *some* apparently totally withdrawn children *may* respond to consistent and contingent use of attention-deprivation.

MASTURBATION

The practice of masturbation is typical in young children and its significance is usually grossly exaggerated. Parental attitudes and social taboo concerning it contribute to distorted notions about sexual activities in general, often resulting in unnecessary guilt over this altogether natural activity. In some children, conflicts about masturbation cause withdrawal into obsessive indulgence—and that practice is unlikely to be altered by punishment, criticism, or rejection.

In private conferences, the child who masturbates must be helped to understand where and when the activity will cause negative social repercussions. The student, already being well aware of his habit's unpleasant impact on others, is generally eager to cooperate with any practical method he can use to eliminate it; however, care should be taken to impress upon him that the only unhealthy consequences of masturbation are the discomfort and antipathy it creates in others.

The target behavior can be stated, "I will keep my hands above my desk." Start reinforcing the child for maintaining the behavior over short periods, at the same time supplying him with a large variety of constructive activities to keep his hands occupied. As progress is shown, time periods can be lengthened and the child will begin to replace masturbation with the alternative activities that are bringing him more positive social satisfactions.

CLUMSINESS

Some children with no discernible problems in vision or hearing and no physical impairments nevertheless fail to progress beyond early developmental stages in terms of clumsiness. They manage to gain only limited control over body equilibrium, avoidance of obstacles, and handling of utensils and tools. When constantly referred to as clumsy, these children are apt to suffer from embarrassment that causes the characteristic to persevere. For this reason, avoid scolding a youngster for spilling food, falling down, or showing other indications of awkwardness. A two-way approach to the problem, which helps most youngsters gain self-confidence and physical balance, is illustrated in a case history.

The report received by his special classroom teacher described Chris as "unable to walk across a room without falling" and "unable to maintain a grip on eating utensils, papers, pencils, or books." A previous visual defect had been remedied and the child had no known neurological impairment.

Observing that Chris walked with a lurch, also that his foot gear consisted of heavy combat boots, the teacher asked his parents to have the boy fitted with lightweight shoes that could be tied securely. Each morning, the teacher checked to make sure his shoes were tied, and each day either the teacher or an aide helped the boy to practice walking in the hall, concentrating on a step-by-step placement of feet. Chris's lunch was brought to the classroom daily while he was learning to discriminate between finger foods and utensil foods and the proper handling of eating equipment.

At the beginning, Chris was consistently rewarded for demonstration of new skills as he learned them, but his personal satisfaction in learning how to manage his body movements soon made extraneous compensations unnecessary.

STUTTERING

Stuttering and stammering should be brought to the immediate attention of a school speech therapist or consultant. Your approach to the child's problem, when it threatens to interfere with the student's performance, should follow advice offered by the specialist.

Whenever a child with speech difficulties reads orally, recites, or speaks in class, resist normal impulses to say words for him and encourage his classmates to remain silent. On the other hand, it is seldom expedient (or helpful to the child) to abandon him when he is obviously locked in a losing struggle to express himself. A direct but casual attack on the word, during which you sound out each syllable or each letter symbol, gives the student essential practice in verbalization before a group. Cooperating with the youngster's efforts eventually reduces his self-consciousness; it is kinder and more practical to offer your help than it would be to exclude him from verbal exercises, to speak for him, or to maintain silence when he is making a valiant effort at communication.

Many speech-impaired youngsters in special classrooms have hearing impairments that have been corrected by appliances. These children, previously accustomed to being outsiders during conversational exchanges, often as a matter of habit exhibit characteristics attributed to withdrawn individuals. A discussion of behaviors stemming from hearing impairment can be found in chapter 8. In cases in which withdrawn behavior is based on emotional withdrawal combined with faulty hearing, helping the child gain trust in his environment should be your first goal.

7

DECEPTIVE BEHAVIORS

Tartuffe (to Elmire). Your scruples can easily be removed. You are assured of absolute secrecy with me and the harm of any action lies only in its being known. The public scandal is what constitutes the offence; since sinned in secret are no sins at all.

MOLIERE, *Tartuffe, act 4*

Obviously, someone who knowingly breaks the law has some flaw of character or of judgment or of sensitivity to right and wrong. Yet I think, too, that if we consider how many people broke the law in the Watergate affair, men who were usually model citizens in their private lives, we must ask if our failures do not somehow reflect larger failures in the values of our society.[1]

JEB STUART MAGRUDER, *An American Life—One Man's Road to Watergate*

1. Jeb Stuart Magruder, *An American Life–One Man's Road to Watergate* (New York: Atheneum, 1974). pp. 317-318. Reprinted by permission of the publisher.

All forms of deceptive behavior appear to be based on the transgressor's assumption that he can trick other people into believing he is innocent of duplicity. We instinctively attempt to protect our self-images, to preserve our dignity, and to avoid punishment by using what we call white lies. We all try to gloss over our own inadequacies and exaggerate our own virtues when dealing with ourselves as well as with others. Only when we are free to recognize that total openness and honesty are part of a perfectionist dream can we accept our personal imperfections without guilt and also tolerate weakness in others.

Most children succeed remarkably in adapting to a set of standards for honesty that the average adult finds impossible to meet in everyday life, especially considering the fact that adults expect more consistency in this regard from youngsters than they are able to achieve within themselves. ''Don't do as I do—do as I say'' expresses the hope of each generation that its young will somehow manage to achieve blemishless perfection.

As a teacher, you can point to examples of honest behavior and help your students understand the advantages of being consistently trustworthy. Nevertheless, you are wise to remember that, in most cases, lying, stealing, and cheating are behaviors that can be interpreted as rebellion against authority, as compensations for deprivation of love or material needs, or as efforts to become accepted in a group.

UNTRUTHFULNESS   If you can lead a child who is habitually untruthful into recognition of the reasons for his lying, he'll be better prepared to deal with realities he formerly felt compelled to avoid. We lie to make others feel better or to escape telling truths others would find unpleasant. We lie to avoid awkward situations, to help a friend save face, to save personal dignity. We find it easier to use a headache for an excuse than to admit unwillingness to attend a meeting; we praise the boss's ideas while privately believing them to be stupid.

The use of trivial deception seems to make day-to-day existence infinitely less complicated than absolute honesty would make it; common courtesy often demands such deception. Therefore, lying, like many other things in life, is harmful only when misused or when not used in moderation. Children are admonished never, never to lie, but this is contradicted by what they see in actual practice. Children who learn to be "truthful" have merely learned to judge the difference between necessary lying and lying that is either useless or destructive.

A student who repeatedly lies out of fear of punishment, or because he wishes to win admiration, should be made aware that his attempts at delusion are transparently obvious—that they are not serving their intended purpose. The "mistake" can be called to the child's attention without indication of judgment or disapproval. Once he begins to feel accepted as he is, he tends to lose the need to embellish or alter the truth.

Some children make up stories to divert suspicion from themselves and direct it to one or more classmates. Lessons demonstrating the unjustness of this practice can be brought out in role playing and class rap sessions for developing sensitivity to the feelings of others.

Lying based on pure fantasy is most easily dealt with by bringing up discussions of the difference between real and made-up stories. It is all right to play along with a fantasy if you let the child know that you, too, are pretending. Use of an active imagination is to be encouraged, but children must be made aware that their fantasies belong in this category.

PATHOLOGICAL LYING

The child who is permitted to lie habitually without being challenged or who becomes skillful at making others accept his statements as truth may not learn the devastating effects of the habit until it is too late for him to comprehend the difference between truth and falsehood. It's possible that a young child's pathological lying could stem from a neurological irregularity. Prognosis for therapy of children exhibiting the behavior is unfavorable in any school situation, because it requires more time and attention than a classroom teacher can give.

Sandy, a senior in high school, had a long history of many varieties of delinquent behavior but would never admit anything. She invariably came up with a logical alibi, presented in a convincing, straightforward manner. Her clear eyes were unwavering, her face solemn and earnest, and her declarations of innocence studded with moral platitudes as she answered charges. Even when teachers and principals were virtually certain of her guilt, she repeatedly talked herself out of predicaments by which her position as a popular leader of her peers was threatened.

Finally, during her senior year, Sandy's house of cards collapsed. Several schoolmates, frightened by an investigation of drug traffic at the school, implicated Sandy as the key contact and told where the drugs were hidden. Faced with the confiscated materials and the other students' testimony, Sandy swore that her reason for becoming involved had been to expose the drug ring. She was able to persuade authorities that, had they waited a week longer, she would have come to them with the evidence; and she received a probationary release.

During the above developments, several sessions the school psychologist had with Sandy revealed that she had several strong symptoms of pathological lying. The girl's parents rejected the psychologist's recommendation that expert counseling be sought, insisting they trusted their child completely. Sandy was withdrawn from school by her insulted parents.

STEALING

Respect for others' property is not an innate quality; it's necessary for children to learn the difference between "yours" and "mine." Stealing behavior can be motivated by actual want or necessity, curiosity and venturousness, or psychopathic tendencies that require highly specialized treatment. In the majority of school thefts, attitudes demonstrated by teachers and other supervisors play a crucial role, with humiliation and chastisement of the pilferer being infinitely less effective than objective confidence in the child's capacity to develop ethical awareness. Guiding a youngster who appropriates others' property to empathize with theft victims (leading him to replace selfishness with concern for others) is a subtle process that cannot take place overnight, but sensitive handling of every problem of suspected theft will eventually foster a classroom spirit that recognizes property rights of individuals.

Elementary school children respond well to a technique that makes a game of helping a classmate retrieve lost property.

A teacher who was reasonably certain an item reported lost had actually been stolen announced to the class: "Mandy has lost her big black marble—her favorite, most precious one—and I'm sure we would all feel better if it came back to her. Let's all put our heads down and close our eyes very tightly, and concentrate for five minutes on making the marble come back to Mandy."

When the timer rang after five minutes, the marble had "miraculously" appeared on Mandy's desk. Although the teacher knew and felt sure the students knew who had returned the marble, emphasis was placed on sharing Mandy's delight in getting it back. The stigma of theft was not even implied and the culprit was able to return the marble without losing face.

Critics of this approach to the problem of stealing consider it soft and unrealistic. We have been taught to come down hard on anyone who appropriates property belonging to others and we learned the lesson even before we understood the moral principle behind it. Youngsters in your class are old enough to know that stealing is a despised act, that a thief is the object of contempt—yet this does not prevent some of them from stealing. It might be argued that allowing a child to return an item he has pilfered, without letting him know you are aware of his wrongdoing, would give him the idea that he can get away with stealing; but that isn't the point. Anyone can get away with stealing. People who don't steal are sometimes tempted to do so, but they refrain from it because they have intellectualized their own reasons for not doing so. A very small percentage of them have intellectualized only their fear of its consequences, but most of them have embraced ideas derived from the attribute known as conscience, which is a positive, self-governing force based on moral values. A child who has stolen something is more receptive to learning ethical awareness if spared humiliation than he would be if shame and punishment were directing all his attention to his own feelings.

Discovering the key to the room's supply cabinet was missing, the teacher first asked all students to help search for it. When the key was not found, the class was told, "Unfortunately, we can't use the tape recorder today because the key to the cabinet has disappeared. Until the key is found, we won't be able to use any of the supplies in the cabinet."

Before the day was over, Lowell told the teacher privately, "I know where the key is. It's in the pocket of the jeans I wore yesterday."

The teacher praised Lowell for considering the value of the materials in the cabinet to everyone in the class, adding earnestly, "I'm very glad you told me about this." Later, as the children were preparing for dismissal, the teacher announced, "I have a feeling the key will appear as if by magic tomorrow." The key was back the next morning.

In finding the courage to admit a rash act, Lowell demonstrated that he had developed confidence in the teacher and the class. Had he seen others upbraided for taking things, his fear would have prevented recovery of the key. Even if he had been found out and punished, that result might have merely increased his craftiness.

Actually, practical experiences, as illustrated by these examples, combined with discussions in class rap sessions about making choices have proved to be more effective than either chastisement or moralizing lectures. Role-playing situations in which one student has a chance to steal from another, to rip off store merchandise, or take advantage of a clerk's error stimulate children to empathize with theft and robbery victims and lead them to discover the logic of practicing fairness and honesty.

CHEATING

There are people of all ages whose standards seem to deny that there is anything intrinsically wrong with deceptive behavior and that the only mistake lies in getting caught. Traditional education uses constant and strict monitoring, repeated warnings and lectures, embarrassing public exposure, and stringent punishment in attempting to eliminate deception. It has been shown repeatedly that these methods tend to reinforce stealth in maneuvering to get by with the very behaviors the teacher is trying to eradicate.

When such restraints are withdrawn, when children are trusted instead of being suspected, the whole atmosphere of a classroom gradually changes. It doesn't happen overnight, but children who are expected to behave with honesty will eventually discover that when they cheat, they cheat only themselves.

Let your students take the responsibility of correcting their own papers. Rather than criticizing them for wrong answers, commend them for working hard and for trying. Their desire to produce correct responses won't diminish; rather, they will become free to evaluate their work realistically, without risking accusations that they have cheated, and to strive for improvement through self-generated effort. If learning, instead of achieving grades, is made the goal, students can realize that cheating to get higher grades fails to accomplish the true goal.

The following article in support of this attitude is used with the author's permission.

LET THEM CHEAT

By Chick Moorman

We're cheating kids by not letting them cheat.

Absurd? Ridiculous? Maybe not. It could just be that the best way to deal with cheating is to allow it to occur. Let's take a closer look.

It's my view that cheating (copying answers, using someone else's paper, etc.) is destructive, self-defeating to the individual as well as to the atmosphere of a classroom, and therefore highly undesirable. It's also my view that many attempts to prevent cheating are undesirable. Here's why.

One method of cheat-control is to employ various ideas, programs and strategies designed to head off cheating before it occurs. Some examples of cheat control include:

1. Arranging desks so that students cannot see another child's paper.
2. Walking around in the room, making comments such as, "Keep your eyes on your own paper."
3. Having kids exchange papers before correcting them.

The height of the cheat control syndrome is exemplified by the teacher who boasts, "Nobody cheats in my room!" and nobody does, supposedly. But that's another issue.

Without question, it is possible for a teacher to impose cheat prevention techniques on children and reduce the amount of cheating that occurs within a classroom. The relationship can be described simply as more cheat control equals less cheating. The equation is basic and it works.

Superb cheat control techniques can go a long way towards preventing the covert act from happening. And the cheating, if not eliminated, will certainly remain under control as long as the control remains. But cheat prevention control is an outer control, coming from a source other than from within the child. It is the type of control that, in order to be maintained, must be rigorously and constantly enforced. A measure of its effectiveness is only a "back turn" or a "leave the room" away.

By controlling cheating in our classrooms, we are programming kids to look to us for control. We are teaching them that we, the authorities, are responsible for their behavior. We are ignoring the lessons of self-assumption of responsibility on the part of the learner. We are passing up opportunities to teach for independence and self-control. We are cheating children.

Children lose because they've missed a chance to grow. They lose again because they pick up a false message. They begin to see others as having control over their lives. They see others as being responsible for their actions. They see it. They learn to live with it. And they grow safe in the protective shell of not taking responsibility for themselves.

Far better to forget cheat control as a preventive practice. It is precisely the prevention of the act of cheating that prolongs the situation by keeping it underground, out of sight and unresolved.

As an alternative, give kids opportunities to cheat. Let them correct their own papers. Create tasks that are self-checking in nature. Post answer keys on the wall. Leave the teacher's edition at the resource table.

Begin by assuming *no one* will cheat. Know that *some probably will*. Kids have been taught well the importance of right answers. Many have their sense of worth connected with it.

When cheating barriers are dropped, some kids will cheat. (Did we really expect anything else?) Those children are not cheating because they are bad, or even dishonest. They are cheating because they haven't learned to feel responsible for their own actions. They haven't realized the difference between the beauty of learning and the insignificance of "right answers."

Once cheat control is ended, kids will begin to communicate their need for growth. Spotting kids who need help is not difficult. Those who usually have little trouble with daily pages or learning center tasks, but then stumble on check-ups and evaluations, are telling us something. Others will be more obvious.

Once the "cheaters" are identified, we can begin to assist in their growth. We can start by accepting them as they are, without judgments, while trying, at the same time, to lead them to new plateaus of thinking and operating. And we can set the example of stressing the flavor of learning while reducing the emphasis on rightansweritus.

We must break away from our need to showcase our values and create "examples." When we need to confer with a student, we can do it in private, respecting the child's fallibility and humanness. We can make direct observations, stating what we see happening, while sharing our concerns honestly. Our emphasis can be positive and supportive. We can help students set goals and develop action plans in *independent behavior* the same way we provide direction in math and spelling.

Most of all, we can control how we view cheating. When cheating occurs, it is possible to look at it from varying perspectives. We can view it as disgusting, dishonest, and immoral and react by imposing regulations to prevent its reoccurrence. Or, we can see cheating as a statement of need for growth and react as if it were an opportunity for learning to take place. The choice is ours. How we choose to view cheating must reveal to kids something of ourselves as teachers as well as human beings.[2]

DEVELOPING TRUST

A teacher must keep constantly in mind that, if mutual trust is to be practiced in the classroom, it is supremely important that the teacher live up to students' expectations. If you make an answer book available, you cannot show disapproval when students appear to make exorbitant use of it. When you confiscate a toy someone has brought to school and is using during a work session, make sure that toy is returned to the student to take home. If you issue a warning that you will keep a forbidden article until the end of the school year unless it is taken home, then the item appears at school again, make good your promise. An announcement such as, "We can fingerpaint when we have finished social studies," means the teacher will not let social studies last so long that no time is left for finger painting.

Clearly defined rules have maximum value in assisting a teacher to establish an atmosphere of respect and fairness for everyone. If you keep your word, you can validly expect your students to live up to their agreements.

---

2. Chick Moorman, "Let Them Cheat," *Alternative* (Kalamazoo, Mich.: Inservice Education Division, Kalamazoo Valley Intermediate School District) 4, no. 2 (1974), p. 1. Reprinted by permission of the author.

8

BEHAVIORS STEMMING FROM PHYSICAL IMPAIRMENT

Mr. and Mrs. Jockimo [Paul's parents] *decided years ago that no matter how hard it might be for them to make demands of Paul, the future would be easier for him if he learned to do as much as possible for himself.*[1]

BERNARD WOLF, *Don't Feel Sorry for Paul*

1. From *Don't Feel Sorry for Paul* by Bernard Wolf (New York: Lippincott, 1974), p. 11. Copyright © 1974 by Bernard Wolf. Reprinted by permission of J. B. Lippincott Company.

In the face of their own feelings toward a physically handicapped child, combined with emotions shown by relatives, friends, and neighbors, few parents find the stamina to place their child's need for independence in first priority. Resisting constant temptation to do things for a disabled youngster and controlling natural impulses to display pity for one who is struggling to overcome a handicap require a special kind of strength that demonstrates respect for the child's basic right to become as self-sufficient as possible. Such respect reaches beyond sympathy and it frees the impaired child to claim his or her full share of autonomy through efforts that only the child can make.

When a physically impaired student is also emotionally impaired, his behavior problems almost always relate to his conflicts between the natural need for independence and the limitations imposed by his handicap—compounded by his reactions to the attitudes of other people. As a teacher of emotionally impaired youngsters, you cannot ignore any physical impairments that might be involved; neither can you allow a child to use physical disability as a refuge from the real world in which he or she must learn to function. A child accustomed to being pampered and helped a great deal may consider you cruel when you make difficult demands of him, but after he begins to take pride in achievements he previously thought to be impossible, he'll probably appreciate your guiding him toward independence.

COMBINING
OBJECTIVITY AND
SUPPORT

Most physical impairment carries a double handicap: the abnormal function itself and social attitudes toward it that can range from sentimental oversolicitude to loathing and avoidance. The greatest difficulty in helping a physically impaired child to achieve maximum performance lies in guiding him to a realistic acceptance of his situation. Allowing him to retreat into self-pity or to use his disability as an excuse for failure will rob such a youngster of opportunities to develop the extra measure of courage he must acquire to live comfortably with his impairment. At times, this necessitates displays of optimism on the part of a therapist that may appear unrealistic; however, no person should ever be limited by another's judgment of his abilities. Every child has the right to the chance to grow. Those who have been stunted deserve chances to overcome any negative opinions that may have contributed to inhibiting their growth.

However helpless an impaired youngster may appear to be, you never know what he can or cannot accomplish until you have given him plentiful opportunities to try the impossible. Obviously, you cannot teach a deaf child to hear or an irreparably crippled one to walk, but you can and must encourage both youngsters to accomplish everything they possibly *can* do; and, if you're bold enough, this involves abilities that diagnosticians (or you yourself) may have considered nonexistent.

In the course of gathering diagnostic information on Jean, a nine-year-old blind girl, the special education office of a school district received the following letter from a neurosurgeon.

"Jean is about as pitiful a case as you have ever seen. She came to [this] hospital after having gone blind rather suddenly . . . an air study was carried out which showed a tumor in the region of the hypothalamus . . . though she was given X-ray therapy . . . there was no change in her condition.

"She has good reason, for all of her symptoms are on an organic basis. I am sure the psychological element enters as well but I believe that from a teaching standpoint you can do nothing. . . . I do not wonder that you have had such a bad time with this child. . . . I doubt that there is any use of Jean's going to school as far as learning is concerned."

Jean had been blinded at age eight, and at least a year of schooling had already been lost by the time she was placed in a special classroom for emotionally impaired children. After three years there, during which she and her teacher received regular services of a special consultant for the blind, Jean currently writes on a braille typewriter; reads braille at third-grade level and does math in braille at fourth-grade level; has a listening comprehension at sixth-grade level; retells television and film stories she has "watched"; finds her way alone around the entire school building and parts of the playground; participates in physical education classes; swims; and goes horseback riding every Saturday.

Physically, Jean is obese and she tends to grow lethargic in the afternoons. It's possible that some of the lethargy may be a result of Jean's program of heavy medication.

The child still balks at trying new activities, possibly at least partially due to parental overprotectiveness in her home environment.

The combination of empathy and relentlessness that is required in successful therapy is understandably difficult for parents of physically impaired youngsters to attain. First of all the parents' original trauma at the time impairment is discovered or injury sustained is among the most complex of painful experiences. Typically, it engenders conflicting emotions that include grief, sympathy, shame, and guilt; and the family's struggle to adjust to a physically impaired child inevitably influences the child's behavior patterns.

In addition, even a youngster whose parents have surmounted emotional obstacles must endure the stares of strangers, ridicule from other youngsters as well as countless other forms of thoughtless treatment inflicted by the public, by friends, and by relatives outside his immediate family.

Whatever attitudes an impaired child has lived with in the past shape his reactions at school, and he'll attempt to cling to any dependency he has developed regarding his disability. Some classroom problems associated with specific physical impairments will be taken up in this chapter.

HEARING
IMPAIRMENT

Rooms for emotionally impaired children sometimes include students also diagnosed as hearing impaired whose hearing problems have been corrected by surgery, appliances, or both. Such children should be receiving regular therapy from speech and hearing specialists, but many haven't learned the habit of wearing and using their hearing aids. Your first problem with a hearing-impaired child is to make certain he is taking full advantage of his hearing appliance; since he can turn it on or off at will, he may need special encouragement to listen to you and to his classmates. Persons long accustomed to deafness are sometimes irritated by sounds and lapse back into non-participation or their former dependence on reading lips. Since your main goal with a hearing impaired youngster is to establish communication and develop his speech skills, it is necessary for him to learn the speech sounds that go with lip movements and to reproduce them. During the transition stage, you may be required to use some signing, gesturing, and writing, but such props should be accompanied by full verbal expression and should be phased out as rapidly as possible.

SPEECH IMPAIRMENT

It has already been mentioned that the speech-impaired student should be receiving help from a speech correctionist; however, the limited training time must be supplemented by hours of practice. The child's speech therapist should share information with you and answer your questions about the child's particular problems.

In general, advice given in chapter 6 under the topic of stuttering is applicable to all speech difficulties in the classroom. The sooner you openly recognize and routinely accept a speech impairment in one of your students, the sooner the student and his classmates will also take it in stride. The most important quality you can demonstrate, in addition to openness, is patience in helping the student practice enunciation. Since there is a definite relationship between speech and reading skills,[2] self-confidence in verbal communication is essential to optimum educational achievement.

BLINDNESS

Now that totally blind children are being integrated into regular education in some parts of the country, it is probable that your class will occasionally include one or more blind students. These youngsters have learned (or are learning) braille from a special consultant whose duties advisedly include supervision of academic work that requires braille. You are furnished copies of the lessons in conventional writing, which enables you to help the student prepare his assignments.

Make it possible for a blind student to participate in classroom activities by devising special materials when necessary. Cloth of varying textures can be glued to game pieces; Quizmo and other game cards are available in braille; easily identifiable sizes and shapes can be used in token economy. When a film is shown, an adult supervisor or another student can sit beside the blind child and quietly describe it without disturbing others. Your school library or resource center can supply braille magazines, braille books, and recordings for the blind, many of which duplicate the content of media being used by sighted students.

As in other areas of physical impairment, the blind child's attitude toward himself is all-important. Deprived of visual contact with his environment, the blind person easily becomes self-centered, uncommunicative, and overly dependent on others—traits that can be counteracted by systematic stimulation of his remaining senses. If the child is to achieve his maximum capability, he must learn to function as independently as possible in a sighted society.

Include your blind student in all class discussions and give him as many chances to recite orally as you give his classmates. Expect his participation in recess, physical education, and other physical activities as a matter of course. Start with mobility orientation inside the classroom, first teaching the child to distinguish left from right if necessary, and praise the student generously for each bit of progress in learning his way around the room without help.

At first, it may be necessary to guide the child's every move. If there is no consultant available to help with mobility orientation practice, make it a point to learn the few techniques you need for the task, such as how to walk with a blind person and how to give the hand signals commonly employed. You or an aide should conduct the child to the washroom, cafeteria, library, playground, and bus boarding area—but, from the

2. Samuel A. Kirk, *Educating Exceptional Children* (New York: Houghton-Mifflin, 1972).

beginning, help should be extended with the aim of teaching the child to reach these destinations on his own. Keeping that aim in mind, encourage the student to assume increasing amounts of responsibility until he gains enough self-confidence to walk short distances accompanied by a fellow student.

You rarely find a child who is unwilling to help a sightless classmate; most children are eager to do so and must be taught to avoid overprotecting the blind. In fact, whenever you get a blind student, his classmates should be instructed on proper techniques for assisting him during his orientation to the class. Giving your students opportunities to help in this way will provide them with positive experiences while reducing the blind student's dependence on adult guidance.

It's difficult to determine at what point a child with no vision is ready to go on an errand to the office unaccompanied or to walk to the washroom on his own. Some youngsters insist on more independence than they can handle; others are extremely fearful of trying anything without help. Since every blind individual must inevitably face countless unfamiliar experiences on his own before he can be liberated from his impairment, a blind child must develop courage to try new activities—but this must be tempered with intelligent acceptance of the realities imposed by his physical limitations. Once he begins to enjoy the release that comes with confidence in his self-management, occasional collisions with obstacles exert diminishing amounts of trauma—and finally are accepted without undue trauma.

Blindisms

Many sightless children exhibit apparently compulsive habits (squinting, grimacing, turning head to one side, eye poking) called blindisms. Like the tics and repetitive gestures seen in other individuals, these habits are amenable to elimination through enlistment of the child's cooperation in: (1) recognizing that the mannerism is unproductive and unattractive, (2) setting target behaviors that seek to eradicate the mannerism, and (3) earning approval and other rewards for accomplishment of target behaviors. An example of successful elimination of eye poking is given in chapter 13 under the heading "Fines."

Partial Visual Impairment

Children with partial visual impairment usually need encouragement to make use of whatever eyesight they have, however minimal it may be. A child with only pinpoint vision, for example, can learn to avoid bumping into things by utilizing his limited ability to see. One youngster, whose vision covered an extremely tiny area, developed the ability to conceptualize a whole object by mentally reconstructing fragments of perception. This boy became able to tell time on the wall clock in his classroom.

Most students with corrected vision—especially if corrections have been recent—have to be helped to take responsibility for wearing their glasses. Some children who are accustomed to being cut off from visual stimulation, upon being encouraged to look at things and describe them, only gradually become aware of the enormous difference the use of glasses makes in their relationship to the world around them. As they learn to depend on vision they come to appreciate the importance of wearing their glasses. Helping a visually impaired youngster realize the value of using his glasses is more effective, and surely more enjoyable, than repeatedly reminding him to wear them.

LEARNING DISABILITY

A child diagnosed as learning disabled should be regarded as one who has not yet mastered academic materials appropriate for his grade level—not as a child who for undiscernible reasons cannot learn. Many so-called learning disabled youngsters wind up in classrooms for the emotionally impaired with behavior problems at least partially stemming from academic failure. In many cases, by setting realistic learning goals for such children and by employing teaching methods described in chapters 9 and 10, you can help this type of student achieve previously unrecognized academic potential. When a child carrying the stigma *learning disabled*—which unfortunately can sometimes be another way of saying unteachable—discovers he actually *can* learn, his behavioral problems are likely to begin dissolving.

EDUCABLE MENTALLY IMPAIRED CHILDREN

It sometimes happens that a child who speaks and acts abnormally and who seems to be a slow learner is erroneously diagnosed as mentally impaired, when in reality he is encumbered by some form of hearing impairment. For that reason, any student you receive who bears the label of mental impairment should be closely observed for signs of hearing disability. If the child turns his head to listen, fails to pay attention a great deal of the time, repeats material inaccurately, slurs his speech or has other speech defects, or exhibits any other clues to poor hearing ability, you should recommend that he be examined by an audiologist.

The term *mentally impaired,* like *learning disabled,* carries connotations that seem to preclude success in teaching a child with that diagnosis. Unfortunately, scores derived from intelligence tests are interpreted to prophesy children's school achievement, with arbitrary minimum and maximum scores designating precise ranges of ability levels. Thus, statistically-derived cutoff points are considered to be so accurate and are accepted so literally that a child's entire future can depend on whether he scores within the range of "dull normal," "educable mentally impaired," or merely "trainable mentally impaired"; and the difference is sometimes determined by a single point on either side of the line. To compound this fallacious use of intelligence tests, the I.Q. score, despite voluminous evidence to the contrary, is still believed by many educators to be a fixed characteristic that like eye color remains constant throughout life.

Dan's teacher referred him to a psychologist for testing because he was failing in all his classes. The teacher was heard to remark to a colleague, "I hope he turns out to be mentally impaired—then I won't have to bother to try to teach him anything."

As a matter of fact, an intelligence test measures only certain aspects of an individual's functioning, in a specific time and place, and under temporary circumstances.

Irene was operated on for kidney failure before being placed in a foster home that offered many advantages over her previous home environment. Originally disgnosed "trainable mentally impaired," she was placed in an educational facility that routinely administered annual intelligence tests. The child's I.Q. score climbed a few points each year.

After Irene was found to have a hearing impairment and was fitted with an appliance, her intellectual curiosity increased dramatically. Further testing placed her in the category of "educable mentally impaired" and made her eligible, at age twelve, for exposure to academic training.

When used as specific indicators of what skills children have learned and of what deficits they have, intelligence tests perform a valuable service. You'll encounter numerous students whose I.Q. scores seem to reflect an accurate appraisal of their individual ability to learn; nevertheless, you should *always* provide every possible opportunity for each child to learn and grow to the limits of his ability. Regardless of intellectual limitations, almost every youngster can learn and retain practical knowledge that will help him to manage his own life in the future

HYPERACTIVITY

It is not uncommon for a hyperactive child to be placed on medication, with no consideration being given to the cause of his hyperactivity. When physical causes such as a glandular malfunctioning or brain damage have been determined, medication can be beneficial in helping the overactive child gain control over his behavior; however, when there is no discernible physical basis, medicine can prove to be detrimental to the child. Since you have no authority as to whether or not a student should receive medication, all you can do in cases in which you suspect medication to be against the child's best interest is suggest to his parents that they discuss the matter with the child's physician; then offer to provide the physician with data (*not* opinions) to help him or her reconsider the need for chemical therapy.

In chapter 4, a hypothetical class-disrupter with symptoms of hyperactivity (Scott) is used in the illustration for techniques in teaching self-discipline. Many youngsters like Scott are voracious for attention and have learned in the past to claim attention through kinds of disruptive behavior, which are then attributed to hyperactivity. Awareness of the youngster's history, combined with a reasonable period of observation and day-to-day relationships with the child, should enable you to determine for yourself whether or not possible physical causes of hyperactivity should be suspected and explored. Aside from social and interpersonal factors that can result in a child's erratic behavior (in addition to brain trauma and glandular imbalance), such things as diet, allergies, and irregular sleeping schedules can cause transient episodes of restlessness and inattention.

EPILEPSY

Occasionally you may encounter a student with a history of epilepsy whose disease has been brought under sufficient control to allow placing him in a school situation. Grand mal seizures are rare when medication is taken regularly; however, some epileptic children learn to simulate a seizure and to use it as a form of temper tantrum. Mild epileptics may never go into convulsions, but undergo intervals of petit mal during which they briefly lose conscious contact with their environment. The latter condition presents no serious threat to a student's overall ability to function in school. Once you learn how to recognize and anticipate petit mal, you can make practical allowances for it without giving it overt attention.

Whenever a child with epilepsy in his history comes into your class, make it a point to prepare yourself mentally for an unexpected seizure. Nothing need be said to the student himself, nor should other members of the class be warned ahead of time. Then, if the time comes that the child suddenly begins to convulse, your most important duty will be to remain calm. Quietly tell the class, "Tom is having a seizure. The best way we can help him is to let him alone. He will get through it, and he will be all right when it's over."

While you are making the above statement, watch the child closely. Authentic grand mal, involving complete loss of control, can cause its victim to injure himself. If the youngster has struck his head against a hard object, seems to be choking, or is in any other severe emergency, follow your school's procedure to get medical help immediately. If he shows no external injury, but is doubled up or lying on his back, straighten his body and turn him on his side, making sure his tongue is in normal position.

After you have taken care of the child's immediate physical needs, go about your business of teaching the rest of your students as if nothing had happened. This is the only thing you can do. The child will recover; and his classmates, after the first experience, will be aware of appropriate measures in coping with a grand mal seizure.

False seizures can be identified after you have discerned that they follow a pattern. Some epileptic children have become so accustomed to commanding attention by means of their illness that they will time their convulsive episodes for occasions such as when the entire school population is passing through the hall. Others will threaten the teacher with warnings such as, "If you say no to me, I'll have a seizure." These behaviors can be dealt with by the methods described for dealing with temper tantrums in chapter 5.

BRAIN DAMAGE

The diagnosis of brain damage is frequently made when a child shows symptoms of perseveration, writing reversals, confusion over directions, and various self-stimulating behaviors that have no traceable etiology. The diagnosis is applied in many cases where physical proof of brain damage has not been demonstrated. Because symptoms presumed to indicate brain damage are usually behaviors that can be altered through learning or relearning, the diagnosis should *not* be taken to mean that the individual's *ability* to learn has been impaired. The human brain has remarkable adaptability. Methodical instruction, broken into small increments of knowledge and combined with patient confidence in the "brain-damaged" child's capacity to grow, has started many a youngster with this label on the way to academic success. (When learning does take place, one might ask whether the brain damage has disappeared or is still present—and indeed question the validity of the diagnosis.) As in most examples of learning disability, it is up to the teacher to explore every possible avenue of approach to each "brain-damaged" student's learning thresholds.

CEREBRAL PALSY

Cerebral palsy victims whose physical impairments do not prohibit their functioning in a school situation may at times be placed in your classroom for development of behavioral goals. Many children with cerebral palsy have high intellectual skills that can lead to their becoming significant contributors to society once they recognize their own capacities and gain self-confidence.

The most difficult handicaps these children encounter are related to the ways they differ from others, plus thoughtless comments and/or treatment they receive from others. Slow, difficult speech, slurring of words, and even the necessity to emit sentences in gasps or squeaks do not make verbal communication impossible—but they do inhibit speech in a youngster who is sensitive to the reactions of listeners. Malformation of hands, inability to hold the head normally, and general lack of physical coordination do not always preclude writing, reading, and body management—but when these activities attract ridicule (or even well-intentioned helpfulness) the cerebral-palsied child can become paralyzed emotionally as well as physically. The most important behavioral goals for such students involve placing priority on their own personal accomplishments, to the exclusion of any attention their physical appearance may receive. A person who is impervious to ridicule, to doubts others express concerning his ability, and to emotional outbursts of sympathy (however sincere) becomes free to reach for total self-reliance despite even extensive physical impairment.

It is imperative that you familiarize yourself with the child's special areas of interest and encourage him to attain excellence in one or more skills. Success builds any individual's sense of worth, and to persons with physical impairment it is likely to represent extremely essential compensation for visible deficiencies that cannot be remedied. From acceptance of his unalterable differences as realities he must live with, the cerebral palsied child can derive extraordinary impetus to become superior in the abilities that remain within his control.

CONCLUSION: LET THEM GROW

Although you won't be called on, as a teacher of emotionally impaired children, to work with great numbers of physically impaired youngsters, any of the types discussed could appear in your classroom. It should be no more difficult for you to maintain objectivity with these youngsters than it would be with students whose bodies are normal but who have behavioral problems that derive from more subtle origins. As a matter of fact, in most cases, the physically impaired child has the advantage of an openly identifiable handicap that he can understand and learn to accept; and helping a youngster to compensate for a discernible deficiency often results in automatic solution of behavior problems.

The benefits derived from refusal to waste sympathy on a child whose first need is to grow in strength, purpose, and achievement are dramatically illustrated in the book, *Don't Feel Sorry for Paul*. In this true story, Paul Jockimo is a seven-year-old who was born with incapacitating malformations of all his extremities. Through a combination of surgery, prosthetic devices, and his parents' determination to let him grow up normally, Paul becomes a public school student and develops many normal skills. At the end of the book, after the boy has won a prize at a horse show, the parent of another child expresses sympathy for Paul to his mother.

Mrs. Jockimo is thoughtful for a moment. . . . Then she says, "You know, Paul's father and I are awfully lucky people. I don't know what we ever did to deserve a son like Paul. . . . If I could have one wish come true, I would wish that Paul could be as happy for the rest of his life as he is right now. I know that when he grows up, a lot of people won't be as concerned with him as we are. But that's life, and I think he'll be ready when those problems come. No . . . don't feel sorry for Paul. He doesn't need it." [3]

3. From *Don't Feel Sorry for Paul* by Bernard Wolf (New York: Lippincott, 1974), p. 94. Copyright © 1974 by Bernard Wolf. Reprinted by permission of J. B. Lippincott Company.

9
TEACHING READING, SPELLING, AND WRITING

I saw the best thing I could do was to get hold of a dictionary—to study, to learn some words. I was lucky enough to reason also that I should try to improve my penmanship. It was sad. I couldn't even write in a straight line. . . .

I spent two days just riffling uncertainly through the dictionary's pages. I'd never realized so many words existed! I didn't know which words I needed to learn. Finally, just to start some kind of action, I began copying.

In my slow, painstaking, ragged handwriting, I copied into my tablet everything printed on that first page, down to the punctuation marks.

I believe it took me a day. Then, aloud, I read back, to myself, everything I'd written on the tablet. Over and over, aloud, to myself, I read my handwriting.

I woke up the next morning, thinking about those words—immensely proud to realize that not only had I written so much at one time, but I'd written words I never knew were in the world. Moreover, with a little effort, I also could remember what many of those words meant. I reviewed the words whose meanings I didn't remember. . . .

I was so fascinated that I went on. . . . With every succeeding page, I also learned of people and places and events from history. . . . That was the way I started copying what eventually became the entire dictionary. . . .

I suppose it was inevitable that as my word base broadened, I could for the first time pick up a book and read and now begin to understand what the book was saying. Anyone who has read a great deal can imagine the new world that opened. Let me tell you something: from then until I left that prison, in every free moment I had, if I was not reading in the library I was reading in my bunk . . . months passed without my even thinking of being imprisoned. In fact, up to then, I had never been so truly free in my life.[1]

Autobiography of Malcolm X

1. Alex Haley and Malcolm X, *Autobiography of Malcolm X* (New York: Grove Press, 1965), pp. 172-173.
Reprinted by permission of Grove Press, Inc. Copyright © 1964 by Alex Haley and Malcolm X; © 1965 by Alex Haley and Betty Shabazz.

One of the most rewarding experiences a teacher can have is to watch a former nonreader discover the delights of being able to interpret printed words. Children who move from reading failure to even limited success in reading may not verbalize their elation over the new-found skills, but their complete change in attitude toward schoolwork speaks for itself.

Almost every student who has been diagnosed emotionally impaired will exhibit some deficiency in the area of reading and spelling. Anyone planning to teach such children must be aware of the general types of deficiencies and of methods for correcting them.

TYPES OF
DEFICIENCIES

Some youngsters read silently with fair comprehension, but are terrified of being asked to read orally, so retain virtually nothing of material they have been required to read aloud. The child who is constantly helped and corrected during oral reading tends to become increasingly self-conscious as well as overconcerned about individual words. Such a child does not learn to think about what he is reading or to group words into meaningful phrases until the embarrassment he feels about the act of reading aloud is replaced by self-confidence and enthusiasm for the subject matter.

At the other extreme, you find students who have mastered the techniques of decoding words and have become rapid readers in the technical sense—without learning to comprehend the material. When questioned, these word-callers will give ridiculous answers and wild guesses about what has just been read.

Since reading and spelling are basic to all academic work, their mastery should be treated not as an end in itself, but as the ability to handle basic tools for learning and communicating. Children learn easily that letters represent sounds and that combinations of letters form words. To broaden their understanding of the reading process, remind them that words stand for thoughts, images, and things. It follows that when words are written, they still symbolize their meanings—but only when someone reads them and translates them back into thoughts, images, and things. By asking students to name words from their own vocabularies, then showing them what the words look like in writing, then asking them to read those words, you can dispel some of the fear and mystery with which many reluctant readers regard the printed page.

This idea is so elementary that it is often overlooked by adults, particularly those who learned reading and writing easily as children. Some of your students come from homes in which very little reading is done, in which nobody reads aloud to the children, and in which no children's books are to be found. Semiliteracy, actual illiteracy, and (in cases of immigrant parents) scant exposure to the English language are in the backgrounds of many children experiencing school difficulties. Their early reading failures, plus the realization that they are falling farther and farther behind their classmates, tend to generate emotional reactions that compound their academic problems.

FIRST STEP IN
REMEDIATION

Students enter your room bearing a variety of labels that attempt to reflect measurements of their reading and spelling levels, degrees of learning disability, and other terminology designed to pinpoint weaknesses and strengths. It is well to consider test reports, but certainly it is unwise to regard them as infallible testimonials of what a child can or cannot do. The place to start remediation is with your own assessments of the whole child—not by imposing standardized measurements on him from the outside, but by finding out, directly from him, what he knows and what he needs to learn.

Every individual has interests of some kind. Most children talk eagerly about things they like to do or subjects that fascinate them; even the most withdrawn youngster, given freedom to do so, eventually betrays his interests to an alert teacher. Encouraged to prepare art projects, scrapbooks, or verbal reports on subjects of their own choice, students who usually avoid reading and writing can be led into making a transition to these activities as a part of such undertakings. During the course of developing a self-initiated project, a child grows absorbed in his subject, loses his self-consciousness, and shows the teacher his own unique relationship to reading and spelling tasks.

Stock your room's library with a large variety of high-interest books, or accompany your class on frequent visits to the school library, giving each student full choice of his own reading materials. Allowed no opportunity to decide whether they are going to read, but allowed independent decisions on what they will read, most students will make serious selections.

Show interest in their selections. Even when a child has chosen a book that is obviously the easiest he can find, praise him on the *topic*, and when he has read it, discuss the contents with him earnestly. (If the book is far below his interest level, he'll tend to choose more thoughtfully next time.) In other words, make *meaning* the reason for reading. Once a child discovers that reading has something in it for him, speed, accuracy, comprehension, proper eye sweep, and all other reading skills will become amenable to development.

READING
INSTRUCTION

Use of a standardized, school-adopted reading series is not recommended for students with academic problems. First of all, the familiar format is associated with past unpleasantness, perhaps failure, in the minds of such students. Secondly, the books in such a series furnish a constant reminder of specific reading levels—a matter of exaggerated concern to sensitive youngsters. Your students will, of course, be expected to master reading from the official school series when they return to regular classrooms; those books can be reintroduced to each child after he has gained confidence in his reading ability, when he knows he is being prepared to reenter the mainstream.

At the outset, reading instruction should be done on an individual basis. This may sound too time-consuming, but it can be combined with instruction in other subjects; in any case, five to ten minutes of your undivided attention to each student's reading can yield better individual progress than a full hour of class reading involving all students. After you have assessed each student's reading strengths and weaknesses, you can probably group at least some class members by twos or threes, but at the beginning it's wise to avoid asking any obviously unwilling reader to expose his inadequacies to his peers. (When he has improved his skills and gained confidence, he'll enjoy showing the class how well he can read.)

After guiding the child to a selection of material that you're sure will attract his interest (preferably at a reading level below his assigned one), work with him at a table apart from the group. You may wish to discuss the material beforehand or ask questions that it will answer. If the student resists reading orally, you can start by reading a sentence and then asking him to read it. As the child becomes more at ease with you, he'll grow willing to take the risk of making an occasional mistake—especially if you concentrate on the subject matter instead of stopping him to correct every reading error.

The cardinal rule for teaching oral reading is this: No matter how many mistakes your student makes, correct him only when the mistake would change the meaning of a sentence. As his interest increases, the child will read more carefully to catch details. Pointing out each error as it occurs serves only to distract the reader's attention and to discourage him from continuing his efforts.

Once the child realizes you aren't expecting instant perfection, you can begin coaching him on his most prevalent needs for improvement. After a page has been read, first praise his effort, then show him words skipped or misread; talk to him about slowing down to look at each word; or should his problem be word-by-word reading, give him a strip of paper to use as a liner, explaining that it will help his eyes move rapidly across each line. In most cases, you'll be astonished at the quick and complete response to be derived from these kinds of suggestions, as compared to the frustrations that come from making constant, repetitive corrections.

Word-callers need practice in looking for meaning in what is being read. This not only enhances the value of selecting materials that appeal to individual interest; it makes a preparatory discussion and question session mandatory. Start by asking one question before any reading is done, then ask the child to read the sentence that contains the answer. This can be gradually increased to two, three, and more questions and corresponding sentences—then to full paragraphs, then pages. After the student has learned to read for facts, the prior questioning can be phased out and you can switch to asking him to tell you about the material after he has read it. At this level, it's advisable to stick to facts about the subject rather than ask for any value judgments or "What do you think" questions.

Here again, however, you can be trapped into perpetuating errors by giving them too much attention, as the following case history illustrates.

Martha, who read at the fourth-grade level, was observed to be making more errors during individual reading than she ever had made previously. In an effort to break the girl's habit of word-calling, her teacher was using the reading-to-find-answers method, but after several weeks Martha's responses to questions slipped from slight improvement to being less satisfactory than at the outset. The teacher discussed Martha's recent regression with the classroom consultant and the two decided to analyze the teaching situation in detail.

The analysis revealed that a new, good-looking male classroom aide was supervising the child's reading and spending a great deal of time helping Martha understand each question and answer on which a mistake was made. The aide was showing great patience and concern over errors, but whenever Martha offered a correct response his reaction was to smile, give enthusiastic but brief praise, and go on with the lesson. It developed that a far greater amount of time was being spent on instruction following incorrect answers than was being spent following correct ones.

Mr. Handsome was asked to reverse his procedure—to curtail his attention to Martha's incorrect answers and to spend more time praising her for giving correct ones—and he willing complied. Martha's errors in reading recitation soon reduced significantly, whether she was working with the teacher or with the aide.

Further experimentation, involving a brief period of return to the aide's original method, yielded a second increase in Martha's erroneous responses and verified the fact that extra help, in this case, had been responsible for her first increase in errors.[2]

RECIPROCAL
TEACHING

Reciprocal teaching refers to the practice of utilizing facts taught in one subject to illustrate facts being taught in another subject—which incidentally reinforces learning in both subjects.

Most adults are victims of partitioned education. You may not recall its impact on your elementary learning, but you may still be trying in your own mind to integrate facts from separate-but-related courses such as American literature and United States history, or United States history and European history. On the other hand, you probably regard history, mathematics, and economics as three totally distinct disciplines despite having become cognizant of their inherent interrelationships. As a teacher at the elementary level, you can give students their first glimpse of education as a whole cloth woven of countless interlacing threads.

You can take advantage of interrelationships between subjects, as well as between areas of the same subject, to bring more order and significance to your students' total learning. Children who have been diagnosed emotionally impaired typically have relatively short attention spans, accompanied by limited experience in organizing fragmented pieces of information. By showing how one quantum of knowledge complements another—regardless of whether both belong to the same subject—you can stimulate logical application of knowledge, clarify concepts that might never be retained as isolated ideas, and demonstrate the essential coalescence of all learning. The subject is discussed further in chapter 10.

RELATIONSHIPS
BETWEEN SPELLING
AND WRITING

As might be expected, correlation between reading, spelling, and writing skills during the elementary school years approaches 100 percent. Failing readers are usually reluctant to progress from printing to cursive writing; and their spelling lists show poorly formed letters, written either in faint, chicken-track haste or in labored scrawls that reflect hard pressure on the pencil. These children seem to be utterly confused by the shapes and sounds of letters and their puzzlement is compounded by the varying arrangements of letter combinations that build words.

As Paul Roberts said in his textbook *Understanding English*, "Any

2. Condensation of a report by J. Eric Hayes and Robert P. Hawkins, "An Analysis of Instruction Duration as a Consequence for Correct and Incorrect Answers," Kalamazoo Valley Intermediate School District and Western Michigan University, presented at the 78th Annual Convention of the American Psychological Association, Miami Beach, Fla., September 1970. Reprinted by permission of the authors.

way you look at it, English spelling is a mess. A system which puts up with pairs like *fine* and *sign, no* and *know, smile* and *aisle, through* and *cough* is a system which falls considerably short of perfection. It has been suggested that a reasonable spelling of the word *fish* would be 'gh-o-ti' (*gh* as in *rough, o* as in *women, ti* as in *nation*). . . ."[3]

Conventionally, spelling lessons for elementary grades group words that are spelled alike and also pronounced alike; later, when exceptions to these spellings are introduced, attempts are made to provide rules that will cover (some of) the exceptions. Students who are already mystified by different letter combinations for the same sounds, plus different pronunciations for identical letter combinations, become even more confused when rules purported to cover these situations are laid on them. They are told, "*I* comes before *e* except after *c,*" but in the same breath they are warned, "There are exceptions to every rule"; consequently, many of them have to look up the word *seize* in a dictionary (if they care about spelling it properly) the rest of their lives.

Unfortunately, despite widespread attempts to simplify English spelling by phoneticizing it, traditional spelling prevails—and it must be taught. Neither complaining about spelling inconsistencies nor apologizing for them will make them disappear; and trying to ignore the importance of accuracy in spelling (as many students would prefer) cannot be tolerated by a conscientious teacher. To quote further from Roberts, "Your arithmetic can be lousy, your knowledge of history and economics can be zero, you can be totally ignorant of the difference between a molecule and an amoeba, and still you can get along. But if you can't spell, you are in trouble every time you pick up a pencil. Of all writing errors, none stand out like mistakes in spelling. Dangle a modifier or split an infinitive, and chances are nobody will notice; but spell *separate* 'seperate' and people will call you illiterate."[4]

Since spelling must be taught, its many contradictions and inconsistencies must somehow be dealt with. Of the numerous methods that have been developed for doing this, not one has been found to be adequate; but miraculously the majority of students eventually learn to spell in spite of the methods inflicted on them. With students who have already failed to respond to such methods, spelling and writing instruction can be combined with other teaching in such a way as to avoid (at least during early stages) conventional word lists that tend to isolate spelling and writing abilities from their actual purpose—which is, ultimately, communication.

Some students learn to form letters perfectly and can copy material

3. Paul Roberts, *Understanding English* (New York: Harper and Row, 1958), p. 100. Reprinted by permission of the publishers.
4. Ibid.

flawlessly, with little or no understanding of the words they are writing. Others can learn to spell by rote learning that prepares them for the day's lesson but isn't retained for practical use. For these victims of compartmentalization (most of whom additionally suffer reading difficulties), you must find a way to make spelling meaningful and the writing of words more than an exercise in copying.

SPELLING AND WRITING INSTRUCTION

As in teaching reading, it's best to introduce spelling and writing with emphasis on words that are of interest to the individual student. There are many ways this can be done without taking up too much time; you will discover different opportunities with every class you teach.

Because the techniques developed by Fernald for teaching nonreaders of all ages represent a practical approach to writing and spelling as well as to reading, the Fernald method will be explained and some modifications of it will be discussed.[5] Fernald's first premise is that children learn words from their own vocabularies (especially words that they themselves ask to learn) much more easily than they learn words from prepared lists. Her structured program, refined by UCLA Clinic School for Non-Readers at Los Angeles, lends itself to small group situations but can also be adapted to conventional spelling lessons at the elementary level. Although the method requires working with individuals, the teacher and aide can move from desk to desk as needed because most of the process is handled by the students themselves, once they have been shown the series of simple steps involved in learning a word.

1. The child names a word he wants to learn how to write. (Never reject a word because of its apparent difficulty or simplicity.)

2. Using chalkboard-size cursive writing, write the word on a strip of paper (an eight-and-one-half-by-eleven-inch sheet cut in half lengthwise) with a crayon or magic marker.

3. Demonstrate tracing by going over the letters, at the same time speaking the sounds *of letters and blends (do* not *name letters). Where a letter or letter combination is silent, mention the fact beforehand and then* whisper *each silent* letter *while tracing.*

4. Ask the child to trace and sound the word as demonstrated, using the index finger of his dominant hand, and to continue tracing and sounding until he is sure he can write the word independently.

5. When the child says he can write the word, he turns the slip face down and reproduces it on a sheet of paper, using an eraserless pencil or pen.

6. Ask the child to check his word against the model one. If it is correct, he can proceed to the next word he requests; if not, he repeats

5. Grace Fernald, *Remedial Techniques in Basic School Subjects* (New York: McGraw-Hill, 1943), chap. 5.

the above procedure until able to write the word without error, after crossing out—not erasing and correcting—wrong words.

7. At the end of each session, test each child over his words. Those he misses are to be practiced at the next session before he can name any new words.

8. After a word has been reproduced successfully in three consecutive test sessions, the child files the original word strip in his word box—an alphabetized container that provides easy reference to words he has requested.

Word strips can be cut in advance by students or prepared through use of a paper cutter. Word boxes and cardboard dividers bearing the letter of the alphabet can be constructed by the children. Boxes should be long enough to fit the strips (about twelve inches) and four inches in both width and depth. Cardboard dividers are slightly larger than the word strips and can be cut with protrusions to contain letters or else have labeled tabs attached to them. Preparation of these items can be called a mystery project to arouse curiosity before you explain how they are to be used; or you can announce their purpose as a new way to learn spelling.

By involving simultaneous use of a youngster's visual, auditory, speech, and tactile capacities, the Fernald method increases attention and shortens learning time; and children are eager to read back their own words. Word boxes teach dictionary skills and furnish a record of each child's reading vocabulary. Tracing and pronouncing can be kept to a low murmuring that does not disturb others, and skills learned through it are transferred readily to other reading and writing experiences—thus paving the way for teaching vocabulary from regular school subjects. Most students will abandon tracing, either abruptly or gradually, but a few will cling to the practice with an almost obsessive goal of placing word strips behind every letter in their word boxes.

The superiority of tracing and pronouncing over drills requiring copying and spelling is easily recognized. First, a student told to copy a word ten times may make a mistake in the first or second copy, then proceed to repeat the mistake in all other copies. Second, linking sounds to letters gives phonics practice a concrete dimension that is more meaningful than drill over isolated letters and syllables. Third, in going over pairs of homonyms the student will discover his own memory associations for distinguishing between them (for example, *here* is a part of *there* and *where*; but *hear* has *ear* in it—and *heirs* get *theirs*), which eases the sorting out of such spellings.

Before we discuss modified application of Fernald's principles, consider two cases illustrating these principles' use in individual tutoring.

Case A

Jenny's parents became concerned when she had not begun to talk at age three. When she was four years old, Jenny's parents were informed by a speech clinician, after testing, that the child had probably suffered brain damage that would result in continued slow development. The clinician further stated, "Jenny will never be able to finish high school."

Jenny developed some speech before entering kindergarten at age five-and-one-half. In early grades she experienced severe reading and spelling difficulties. Her writing was slow and labored and her everyday speech slurred, marked by omission of syllables. As time went on, her frustrations over these deficiencies were made worse by taunts from her only sibling, a sister two years her junior whose academic ability was above average.

*Jenny was a twelve-year-old sixth grader when the Fernald approach to reading was introduced to her. The first word she requested to learn—*antidisestablishmentarianism—*required splicing three word strips before it could be written by the tutor; however, after tracing and sounding it nine times, Jenny reproduced it without error. From then on, she learned a rapidly expanding reading and writing vocabulary at racehorse speed.*

Help with spelling and writing assignments came next, with more new words finding their way into Jenny's word box. Later, the tutor listened to the student read history and social studies assignments orally and then questioned her over them.

Improvement in all areas, including speech, became noticeable almost immediately. After about a dozen sessions, Jenny lost interest in her word box but continued to trace and sound some new words, using the method independently after tutoring was discontinued at the end of six months.

After graduation from high school, Jenny completed junior college, accomplishing both with grades slightly below average.

Case B

Ten-year-old Nate, although diagnosed as a nonreader, was doing passing work in fifth-grade math and receiving good marks in oral participation involving other subjects. His mother explained he had been floated through school because his teachers, although consistently baffled by his failure to read and write, considered him very intelligent.

Nate maintained polite but adamant silence while the tutor demonstrated the trace and sound method of learning words and when asked to name "any word you choose" he lowered his head, seemingly paralyzed with embarrassment. The tutor switched lightly to other topics, but every time the subject was brought back to words the child ceased responding. After twenty-five minutes, the tutor suggested that Nate point to a word of his choice on a page of print; at that, the boy grinned self-consciously and murmured the word the *almost inaudibly.*

Sensing that this might be a word Nate already knew, the tutor wrote it out for him with utmost seriousness. Nate attacked tracing and sounding with equal seriousness, going through the process five or six times before attempting to produce the word. He wrote it hesitantly, but correctly.

Within the next half-hour the boy learned three more words, all names of objects in the room: chair, table, picture. *He passed all words on his first review test and repeated this success at the beginning of his second session. This was the beginning of a veritable flood of commonly used words he requested; and his word box filled up rapidly. Within two weeks his mother reported Nate was looking in newspapers for words and calling out words he recognized on the television screen.*

After a month, Nate voluntarily brought schoolwork to tutoring sessions, began reading orally with a great deal of help, and moved his spelling grade from zero to 100 almost instantaneously. He became an average reader (and an above-average student) by the time he entered sixth grade.

Individual tutoring makes it possible to use the final step prescribed by Fernald for each lesson. That step involves giving each student a list of the words he has learned (or the story he has written), typed for him to take home to read to his family. Although it is scarcely expedient to follow this step for a whole class, you should take every possible opportunity to find occasions for exposing your students to their writing in typed form. A newsletter or some other project requiring everyone to contribute will create enthusiasm, and the finished product will be gratifying to your class, as children enjoy seeing the results of their efforts in print and will read them over and over.

In addition, manipulation of such instruments as toy printing presses, rubber stamps with exchangeable letters, stencils of words or letters, and labeling machines can familiarize young children with letter shapes and combinations while holding their interest in word building.

Any number of modifications of the Fernald method of teaching writing and spelling can be utilized. Should you decide that individual instruction is unwieldy or unnecessary, you could use tracing and sounding to teach regular spelling words from the chalkboard. Take the words one by one. After writing the model word on the board and discussing its meaning, lead the class in repeating the sounds while you trace the word lightly and your students "write it in the air." Erase the word; ask the students to write it on their papers; and test over all words at the end of the practice.

If your class would like to build its own spelling lists, you can use the chalkboard method to teach words suggested, making sure that everyone contributes to the list. Or you can help the children find spelling words during the course of science, social studies, or other lessons and teach them when it is time for spelling.

Instead of word boxes, students can prepare small booklets in which to write their own words—or words they have difficulty in spelling—or any category of words that is chosen. Booklets can be alphabetized and even used as personal dictionaries if brief definitions are written in.

The privilege of learning one or more of his own words to preserve in his word file can be used as a reward mechanism, without resorting to any other use of the Fernald techniques. Since many children delight in spelling long or difficult words, this would help to increase their vocabularies; others can be encouraged to concentrate on frequently used words they have found difficult.

You'll be able to devise techniques that best fit your class each year. The main thing to remember is that the teaching of reading, writing, and spelling cannot be placed in separate compartments, each treated as an end in itself. Your job is not so much to teach speed, comprehension, and accuracy as it is to prove to your students that knowing these skills will bring them benefit and enjoyment the rest of their lives.

10

TEACHING MATH, SCIENCE, AND SOCIAL STUDIES

People ask me, "Where do you live?" . . . I answer that I live on a little spaceship called Earth.[1]

R. BUCKMINSTER FULLER

1. R. Buckminster Fuller, *Utopia or Oblivion* (New York: Bantam, 1969), p. 262. Reprinted by permission of the publisher.

Education in the past has treated each subject in the curriculum as if it had some kind of boundaries around it that distinguished it from all other subjects. Admittedly, partitioning of subjects simplifies grading, particularly since the interest and abilities of individual students seem to cluster around different subject areas. However, students' tendencies to prefer certain subjects over others may result at least partially from such arbitrary sectioning of knowledge into separate compartments. It is becoming more and more evident that strong emphasis on individual interest and abilities, to the exclusion of broad general learning, is producing a degree of specialization that results in loss of communication between specialists in different fields and even between specialists within the same field.

Although a diagnosis of emotional impairment may involve some educational impairment, you should never assume that your class doesn't embrace the so-called normal curve of intelligence, I.Q. scores notwithstanding. Given conditions that encourage it, giftedness will surface in a classroom for emotionally impaired fully as frequently (perhaps more frequently) than in populations of normal students. Start teaching with the assumption that every child in your class has untapped capacities; you'll be gratified, as time goes on, to note many unexpected cases of dramatic improvement, as well as a few eruptions of intellect and creativity denoting superior ability.

Reciprocities between reading, spelling, and writing were discussed in chapter 9. The present chapter mentions only a few ways the subject areas of mathematics, science, and social studies—the interinvolvements of which are less evident—can be reciprocally applied in teaching. In addition, the general philosophy of teaching subject matter by using the immediate environment is emphasized.

MATHEMATICS

Methods used in teaching beginning arithmetic make numbers exciting to young children, who usually take pride in learning number symbols and their simplest applications. Later on, numbers appear to grow in complexity and, at the same time, to become increasingly dissociated from everyday experience. Repetitious drills, artificial problems that hold no immediate interest, and constant stress on exact methods for reaching precise answers all fail to sustain the enthusiasm aroused during earlier exposure to the subject of mathematics. Furthermore, since math is typically structured to progress in difficulty within any one year and from one year to the next, a student who loses out on one step in a single grade or who learns little math for a full school year becomes permanently crippled in mathematics unless the gap in his knowledge can be filled through special help.

As lesson schedules move from one process to another, youngsters seldom become aware of the relationships between addition, subtraction, multiplication, and division, and they get only hazy notions of how to apply these processes in their own lives. New math, a system using algebraic abstractions, which was devised in the 1950s to demonstrate concepts behind the processes, drove mathematics curricula further into the realm of symbolism and employed language that baffled teachers as much as students.

But fun with numbers need not be confined to the first year or two of schooling. If you make full use of materials in the immediate environment, you can teach all the math your students need to know to make easy transitions to textbook math as it is presented in regular classrooms.

The teacher of an adult class in remedial math opened the first session by asking students what they wanted to learn. One man, explaining he had lost a job because he could not read the marks on a ruler, asked to be taught that skill. On inquiring, the teacher was surprised to discover that only one person in the class of fifteen—all of whom had attended elementary school—knew how to interpret measurements on a twelve-inch ruler down to the one-fourth-inch divisions.

Mechanical drills over the fundamental principles of any math concept tend to result in memorization that is short-term and without any apparent value to children.

Linear measurement can be taught by using rulers, yardsticks, and tape measures to gauge actual dimensions of familiar objects; then, as the class moves through the same succession of concepts and processes presented in a typical math textbook, a teacher can return again and again to the same fundamental tools for investigation of more complex problems. Meanwhile, the knowledge to be covered by each step can be made visible to students by use of clocks and stopwatches, money, kitchen scales, containers for measuring volume, various kinds of meters, and other tools of measurement, including instruments that provide an intro-duction to the metric system.

During the first week of school, make a class project of finding the height of each child. By the time the measurements are repeated at the end of the school year, some of your students will have learned how to calculate not only amounts of growth but also such things as average rates of growth per month and growth gains (in round numbers) stated in fractions and percentages. Uses of linear measurement can progress to constructing scale maps of the classroom, the school building, and a city block; they also lead naturally into calculations of geometric areas and volumes.

At the beginning, utilize familiar mechanisms of measurement to dem-onstrate basic number sequences and addition. Multiplication by two, four, and eight can be introduced through use of gradations marked on a foot ruler, a kitchen scale, a set of baking spoons and cups; by *five* and *ten*, through a clock face and with nickels and dimes; by *seven*, through a weekly calendar; and by *six*, through a yearly calendar. Since subtraction and division reverse the respective processes of addition and multiplica-tion, the same instruments (or others of your own choice) can be used with them.

Making change for various denominations of money can instill under-standing of fractions and decimals. Comparing how far an automobile and a motorcycle can be driven on a stated amount of gasoline and calculating how far a student travels to school and back in a year are projects that yield answers to interesting questions while they teach processes.

Reciprocal teaching of math and science can take manifold forms, too obvious to require enumeration. Let it suffice to comment that weighing and measuring Jennifer's pet turtle and clocking its speed of travel creates a more memorable experience for Jennifer and her peers than they would get from reading about turtles. As for social studies, math can be applied to comparing populations, disturbances on maps, and statistics on commodities—to name a few possibilities—and it can be used to answer questions such as, "How old was the United States when our state was admitted?" or, "Why do you suppose the numbers system the Arabs invented was based on tens?"

Centering the teaching of math on practical realities doesn't deprive students with above-average mathematics ability, because they are natur-ally inclined to seek answers to challenging problems. Also, they can be given extra assignments in math and, perhaps, can be allowed to join the math period of a regular class in the building in partial preparation for leaving the special classroom. Problems employing theoretical situations and abstract reasoning will be more acceptable to all your students, however, after they have recognized math as a tool for finding out facts they consider meaningful.

Math games providing memorization of facts given in arithmetic tables will be available from your school library or resource center. Varieties of bingo are popular, and there are many others that may appeal to your class. Use of flash cards can be frustrating to slow students, so should be confined to individual students or to groups of near-equal ability. Although memorization of answers to simple math processes is extremely helpful in everyday situations, it is less imperative than it was before calculating machines gained widespread use. Memory for the techniques of addition, subtraction, multiplication, and division enables anyone to arrive at exact answers; all one need know is which keys to press.

SCIENCE

Early in the fall term, take your class on a field trip in search of a caterpillar of the Monarch butterfly or the larva of some other flying insect to be found in your geographical area. Be sure to obtain a supply of the plant on which it was found, as this will be the creature's natural food. If everyone in the class knows how to identify one or more species of caterpillar that would be adaptable to observation, chances of finding a specimen are good; but the trip furnishes other chances to observe nature regardless of whether the main prize is captured. Returned to the schoolroom and isolated behind glass with its food, the caterpillar is on display as it undergoes metamorphosis through pupa and chrysalis stages before finally emerging in the adult stage of its kind.

Monarchs are especially desirable for this type of scientific observation. They breed throughout the northern hemisphere during summer. They accomplish complete metamorphosis in about two weeks, and the newly formed adults migrate each autumn to hibernate on trees in warm southern climates, where they remain from November to March. A source of complete information on this subject is F. A. Urquhart's book, *The Monarch Butterfly*.[2]

In case your school is in a large city or a trip to the country is impossible for some other reason, find a park where some kind of insect can be observed in its habitat, and supplement observation with films showing details of metamorphosis, either before or after the field trip.

Science, both natural and physical, is best introduced to children through immediate experiences and experiments; and the main focus in teaching natural science should be on instilling respect for all living things. Direct examination of different kinds of animals and plants enables a teacher to familiarize students with broad scientific classifications and the characteristics on which they are based without imposing rote memorization.

2. F. A. Urquhart, *The Monarch Butterfly* (Toronto, Canada: University of Toronto Press, 1960).

Make sure all animals collected are set free or returned to where they were found before their lives are endangered. One of the greatest thrills a group of children can share comes at the moment a newly born butterfly is released for its flight back to nature; and releasing wild animals of any kind lends a sense of personal identification that helps youngsters to empathize with their fellow creatures.

Encourage city students to bring turtles, snails, fish—any small animals that can be kept in enclosures—to class for study. If you're near a rural area, extend the invitation to snakes, toads, and other wild creatures. A feeding station attached to a window ledge attracts birds, and, while studying that class of animal, you might be able to hatch some fertilized hen's eggs by incubation.

Plant biology is easily made observable in the classroom with seeds, bulbs, and shoots that serve to demonstrate plant reproduction as well as their growth under different conditions of soil, light, temperature, and nutrition. Naming the parts of plants and their flowers, discussing plant fertilization, and touching upon the rudiments of genetics provide memorable experiences when the subjects are living specimens instead of pictures with printed labels. In the same way, learning names of trees by studying characteristic shapes of their leaves (and the difference between coniferous and deciduous foliage) is more meaningful when real leaves are used.

Natural science can be taken up during fall and spring seasons when specimens are most abundantly available. Remaining months can be spent investigating physical science—rocks, minerals, fossils, shells; the weather; astronomy; electromagnetism and dry cells; simple machines and the principles by which common tools operate. Experiments using many of these things can be set up at the activities center, where they prove to be a popular means of using free time.

Several textbooks and books on specialized areas of science should be kept on hand for constant reference; thus, exercises in reading find broader purpose. A microscope, a bioscope, a telescope, thermometers, and other measuring instruments should be used in experiments that serve to bring math into science class. When social studies involve climate, mines and minerals, forests and uses of trees, agricultural products such as cotton, and various manufactured items, science can be seen to overlap with that subject.

Science should be taught in the elementary classroom by the method of discovery, without rigidly established lesson plans. Lesson plans, of course, are necessary guides for the teacher; but lessons themselves should not be limited to a narrow topic or a set routine. The chance to elaborate on a spontaneous comment or question from the class should always be utilized—but it should be relevant to the subject at hand. (When certain students appear to be trying to distract you from the lesson to avoid scheduled work, offer to take up their questions at a more appropriate time.) As a general rule, remarks contributed by students help to make lessons more meaningful, since knowledge gleaned through personal observation has special value to children; and their world abounds with things to observe.

SOCIAL STUDIES

As in other elementary subjects, the basics of social studies should be taught first. Beyond that, you can guide the class as far as it can go into relevant details. Prepare lesson plans with the aid of several source books and make plenty of reading material (stories about people in other countries) available for students to read.

Start by telling your class, "In social studies, we'll talk about people all over the world," and ask the children to name things that all human beings need to survive. Food, water, and fresh air will be suggested, and, as discussion continued, universal needs for clothing (protection against heat, cold, and other weather conditions) and homes (shelter and comfort) can be listed; and if no one mentions it, you can lead the class to realize that people also need other people.

Rather than concentrating on hemispheres, continents, and political subdivisions, study geographic regions: people living in deserts, with their similarities and differences; people who dwell near oceans and waterways; in mountains; on plains and plateaus; in cities; in frigid zones; in tropics; on islands.

Using fundamental human needs as the central point of departure, you can help children investigate how people in various geographical locations meet those needs. When each different region is introduced, you can return to the same springboard, focusing first on how and why its inhabitants eat certain foods, dress in characteristic ways, and live in their own kinds of dwellings. Photographs, films, and slides provide distinct contrast between living conditions familiar to the students and the climate, topography, vegetation, and animal life found in other parts of the world. From that point, each region can be discussed in depth, continuing to keep the focus on people while their industry, agriculture, customs, and general forms of government are examined.

History, literature, and art of countries in various regions can be presented with the help of curricula in other subjects. For example, the story of ancient Greek culture belongs with Mediterranean studies, and mythology can be taken up as a parallel reading activity. History should be dramatized as much as possible to give it immediate meaning and a "you were there" flavor. If you find ways to vary stories of historical events (such as having students dramatize the coming of the white people to American from the Indians' point of view), children find history quite palatable. With a little research, you can correlate events and contemporaries in different parts of the world. An example is to mention that Galileo invented the telescope at about the same time the first pilgrim colony was founded in North America.

Elementary students should be expected to memorize only a few significant dates in history. Social studies at this level can present a comprehensive view of our planet and people that provides a solid platform for later education—whether that education involves advanced studies or is limited to reading a daily newspaper.

11
COMMUNICATING WITH THE FAMILY

Fiona Farmer was seven years old. Her mother was forty-six, her father was fifty-five, her nurse was sixty-one, and her grandmother and grandfather . . . had reached such altitudes of age that no one remembered what they were. From these great heights Fiona was loved and directed.

She was a pensive child with large attentive eyes and rather elderly manners; all her play was quiet, accompanied at times by nothing noisier than a low continuous murmuring, so it was strange that the rank of dolls on her nursery shelves were scalped and eyeless, like the victims of a Sioux massacre. . . .

(Fiona sneaks out, becomes acquainted with a family of another kind.) . . . Mom stood at the foot of the steps wearing the baby around her neck. Anxiety had made her furious. "That place ain't safe, you know that!" she cried. "How many times have I told you?" She gave Pearl a slap on the cheek and would have given one to Darlene too, if Darlene had not bent her head adroitly.

"Let me catch you up there one more time and I'll get your father to lick you good!"

"Aw, climb a tree," said Darlene.

Fiona was aghast. What would happen now?

But nothing happened. . . . Mom's anger dried up like dew. "You kids want a snack?" she said. "You didn't eat since breakfast."

. . . The table was a family battlefield. Fiona had never seen anything like it before in her life. Stanley and Norman threw pieces of sandwich at each other, Earl took one of Merl's cakes and Merl cried and Mom slapped Earl; Darlene stole big swigs from Pearl's soda bottle, was loudly accused and loudly defended herself.

"You kids shut up," Mom said, eating over the baby's head and giving her occasional bits of cake dipped in tea. . . . [1]

ELIZABETH ENRIGHT, *Nancy*

1. Elizabeth Enright, "Nancy" in *The Moment Before the Rain* (New York: Harcourt, 1951), pp. 179-191. Reprinted by permission of the publisher.

Each child referred to your classroom represents a unique pattern of environmental circumstances, differing in variation and complexity from all other primary environments. The terms *environmental deprivation* and *cultural deprivation* are misnomers. Everyone has an environment, just as everyone shares some kind of social arrangement defined as a culture. Whatever their dissimilarities, the parents of your students have one thing in common: a child whose behavior puzzles and troubles them. Beyond that, each family is as unique as the child it has produced.

Some parents have turned to special education after a desperate search for help from physicians, mental health workers, teachers, and principals. They may complain that they have received little practical advice on how to deal with their child in the home. Typically, these parents are aware of their child's diagnostic label; have accepted, without question, some explanation of the cause of his problems; and may even be reconciled to a pessimistic prognosis that could have been made on the basis of relatively superficial examination.

It would be unwise for you to give parents false hopes or to comment in any way on beliefs that have been adopted during their difficult adjustment to having a "different" child. It is best to concentrate from the beginning on actual steps to be taken at home toward devising a program for the child that is consistent with his program at school. Parents who have tried everything welcome suggestions on definite methods of dealing with their child's most persistent behavioral difficulties and, with sufficient encouragement, they patiently stick to a method until it begins to show results. Informal group sessions for parents or individual conferences for exchanging information and ideas help parents find a sense of direction and set goals for themselves. Students whose parents support your program learn at a faster rate, becoming able to respond appropriately to external controls more easily than those whose parents refuse to become involved. On their part, parents who learn (1) to choose important target behaviors for each child, (2) to practice discipline that provides

freedom within well-defined limits, and (3) to establish clearly understood contractual obligations so the child knows where he stands at all
times tend to develop habits that they find helpful in all family
relationships.

Such parents readily accept specific instructions for dealing with behavior problems in the home, and some even seek chances to observe
your techniques in the classroom. When circumstances warrant it,
methods can be demonstrated to parents in the home.

*Ten-year-old Cindy was termed incorrigible by diagnosticians who
attributed her behavior to an unsubstantiated suspicion of brain damage.
The child had a visual impairment which had been medically corrected.*

*Cindy was a hyperactive, uncoordinated child, who fell frequently. She
engaged in periods of constant running, climbing on furniture, and
making animal sounds. She had a younger sibling, but the entire family
life centered around her. The parents stated they could not entertain at
home, nor could they take Cindy out socially or leave her with a sitter.
They had consulted clinics and physicians all over the state and had been
told that a mental institution was the only advisable placement. In a final
despairing attempt to keep the child at home, the parents sought special
education services.*

*When Cindy was admitted to a classroom for emotionally impaired
children, the teacher privately believed her condition to be hopeless but
decided to begin by involving the parents in the therapeutic process. After
a series of conferences, Cindy's parents agreed to have a classroom
consultant instruct them at home. The consultant modeled methods of
teaching appropriate behaviors and helped set up an isolation area
similar to the one used in the child's classroom.*

*By ceasing to react to Cindy's bizarre behaviors and by adopting
techniques that matched those used in the classroom, the parents assumed
a vital role in therapy. In a much shorter time than could have been
predicted, the child began to change. Within a few weeks, Cindy had
learned to curb her hyperactivity. She stopped falling down, learned to
handle eating utensils, and behaved more rationally. She made
corresponding improvements at school and started to show interest in
academic work.*

*At the end of one semester, Cindy was put in a regular classroom
where she continued to exhibit socially appropriate behaviors and
maintained satisfactory school achievement.*

HOSTILE PARENTS

There are parents of emotionally impaired children who refuse to accept the diagnosis or even to admit there is a problem. They resent their

child's placement in a special classroom and tend to blame the school for whatever difficulties the child is having. This situation can exist even when parents have been fully included in the planning process and have willingly signed the form requesting special education services.

It must be remembered that, regardless of parental attitudes, the natural sense of responsibility felt by parents almost always causes them to carry some degree of self-blame for their child's problems. Whether self-blame and guilt are expressed, repressed, or projected to others, the effect of such feelings is detrimental to the growth of the child. When a parent begins to realize he can contribute to his child's readjustment, he also begins to let go of the past, which holds his guilt. Considering these things, you should make every effort to earn some measure of cooperation from parents who seem hostile toward you.

One of the most effective ways of gaining parental confidence is through frequent feedback on the child's improvement, even when such improvement is minimal. A phone call reporting the most minor behavioral or academic advancement serves to tell the parent you are genuinely interested in the child. The main reason some parents dread telephone calls from school and the reason they avoid teacher conferences is that such contacts often consist of a list of negative reports, which they may interpret to be direct or indirect reflections on them as parents. If you begin on a positive note, and later it becomes necessary to confer with the parents on solving a problem, you'll have established a basis of mutual concern that will negate any supposition that you are merely complaining.

Argumentative parents and those full of resentment against the school are not receptive to logical presentations of opposite viewpoints. You can hear them out without expressing agreement with them (unless you consider their attitudes justifiable); and a remark such as "I'm sorry you feel that way and I'm sure you and I can get along," leaves the door of communication open.

On rare occasions, an unhappy parent may appear at your classroom door, intent on delivering a tirade of accusation and invective for the benefit of everyone within earshot. If this happens, bear in mind that the individual is displaying tantrum behavior and will not respond to reasoning. Keep your temper; make no apologies; say, "I'm sorry you are upset—let's talk about this some time when I am free to discuss it." If the parent has come into the room, go casually to the door and open it, pointing out that your class is waiting now but you will be glad to take time to talk later. If necessary, step outside, then, after the other adult has followed, step back into the room and, while closing the door, repeat, firmly but pleasantly, that you will discuss the matter at a convenient time.

After this kind of an encounter, behave as if nothing had happened. Proceed with your class schedule and make no effort to set up an appointment with the irate parent. However, do make sure to inform your administrator of the incident, so he is aware of it should the parent go to him. In addition, take the first possible opportunity to contact the parent, either by note or a phone call, to report some progress his or her child has made at school. Omit mentioning anything about the previous contact, since by then the parent may be embarrassed at the reminder. Let the matter rest and at your next meeting with the parent extend a friendly greeting to convey the fact that the incident has not affected your relationship with the child.

Uncooperative parents often undergo complete reversals in attitude after new behaviors learned at school begin to generalize to the home situation.

Amy's father ignored her but lavished attention on other children in the family, because he considered the girl a whiner who refused to take part in normal play activities. Amy's teacher tried to convince the father that the child could learn to be unafraid to try new things and to refrain from whining. The father was unimpressed at first, but after Amy began to demonstrate desired behaviors at home he started giving his daughter more attention. Meanwhile, the teacher phoned or sent notes home every time Amy accomplished a new activity. When Amy was returned to her home district after being screened out of the special room, this originally pessimistic parent sent the teacher a plant with a card inscribed, "Thank you for giving me back my daughter."

Failure to appear at a conference, or even an outright rebuff to a teacher's home visit, does not necessarily mean that a parent is hostile. Some adults feel insecure and inadequate, are sensitive about poverty, or have other personal reasons for avoiding a teacher that have nothing to do with their attitudes toward their child or the school. Because your communication with parents is important to the growth of your students, a combination of persistence, courtesy, and directness serves you well in such cases; but it may not always succeed.

Occasionally, for no reason that can be determined, a parent totally resists your every effort to gain home cooperation.

A mother who ignored invitations to conferences at school refused to talk to the teacher at her home, saying she was too busy. The teacher offered to furnish transportation to a conference; the mother said she had to work. The teacher suggested an early morning or evening appointment and even offered to wait for her when the mother gave irregular work hours as an excuse. Finally, after agreeing to keep an appointment, the mother met the teacher's every comment with evasions and rejections.

The teacher's aim was to persuade the mother that her child needed home responsiblities, but she was told, "It's easier for me to pick up his clothes than to make him do it," and, "If he had a pet, I'd be the one who took care of it." Asked for suggestions, she told the teacher to send homework from school. The teacher complied, but the child did not return the homework, reporting, "My mother wouldn't let me do it." He explained he had watched television until it was too late to start the homework, so the teacher sent a note with new homework requesting that it be done at a set time during early evening. The boy brought his assignment the next day with every answer correctly written in–but not in his handwriting.

In this kind of situation, a teacher must simply accept the lack of home support and proceed, without expecting a response, to sending favorable reports to the parents whenever the child shows progress.

PARENT
CONFERENCES

School administrators set times for scheduling conferences with parents. In addition to these regular meetings, it is sometimes necessary to talk to parents on problems demanding immediate attention. Although it takes extra time, both you and the parents can progress faster in helping a child toward his goals if you meet when special questions arise.

Open any conference on an optimistic note, but be honest. The parent knows in advance that his or her child is not perfect, but even casual praise of the child's most attractive feature can put you both at ease for further conversation. If you communicate sincere concern and bring up problems with tact, you gain more cooperation than you could by reading off a list of misbehaviors and bits of advice. Rather than tell a parent he is handling a situation the wrong way, merely suggest that another way be tried and explain the rationale of your own methods. Be sure to discuss the child's positive qualities and also to comment on your appreciation of the parent's cooperation.

Always bear in mind that the parent knows (or at least thinks he knows) his child better than you do. By listening attentively to his point of view, you may gain new insights into the child's environmental circumstances. Without question, respectful consideration for a parent's comments will help you keep lines of communication open between school and home.

CHECK SHEETS AT
HOME

In a limited number of cases, good rapport with parents enables you to suggest their setting up a reward system at home for their child, contingent on an evaluation sheet similar to those used at school (see chapter 3—"Goals"). To avoid making the child feel hemmed in by judgments of his behavior, not more than one or two specific target behaviors should be worked on during a period of time and naturally they should match the youngster's school target behaviors. Each day, parents could offer an incremental reward for appropriate behaviors reported by you plus those observed at home, with weekly rewards proportionally greater and a final graduation or achievement award marking full integration of the new, desired behavior.

Rewards offered by parents can be based on the youngster's favorite activities, food preferences, new toys or clothing, and special trips. Urge parents to keep rewards simple and to link them *definitely* to the fact that they are earned. In addition, stress the fact that more satisfactory results are achieved when parents remember to pay attention to good behavior rather than emphasizing only what the child does wrong.

Use caution in this area. Should a youngster whose parents are keeping a check sheet tell you he has been promised severe punishment at home unless his marks for the week are all ''fair'' or better, this could tend to influence your objectivity in the evaluation process, in addition to negating your emphasis on positive results. Secondly, a student who manages to lose his checklists or who tries to forge parental signatures on them may be signaling that his parents are using harsh punitive contingencies. If discussion with the parents reveals marked inconsistency with your techniques, it would be better to abandon home checklists than to bewilder the child by expecting him to meet separate standards of progress and/or incompatible contingencies.

TEACHING A DOUBLE STANDARD

Whatever your private opinion of a child's primary environment may be, and however it may compare to norms of our middle-class society, that environment represents the youngster's roots and your chances of changing it are negligible. At the end of the school day, the child goes home; you cannot conscientiously send him there with school-imposed behaviors that might make him an outcast in his own culture.

When foul language is an intrinsic part of a student's primary speech vocabulary, learned while he learned to talk and used as a matter of course in family communications, teaching him to reject foul language entirely would be tantamount to depriving him, at least in some measure, of human relationships within his family that are vital to his emotional freedom. By the same token, subjects such as family fights, drunkenness, relatives in jail, observing or hearing sexual activities, and many other topics suppressed or ignored by most people are fully acceptable in some families' daily conversation. Young children from such families experience an initial jolt of wounded perplexity when first exposed to reactions of shock and disapproval concerning such subjects. Some of these children learn rapidly to eliminate language that causes them to be rejected by teachers and the families of their playmates; others seem to thrive on the attention they can get by exploiting it.

To survive emotionally both at home and in the general culture, these children must learn to discriminate between a vocabulary that is appropriate at home and a vocabulary that will serve them advantageously in social situations. Although it is a difficult circumstance to explain without appearing judgmental, if you understand the student's predicament, you can help him to accept a double standard without guilt. Tell him, in privacy, that certain words and activities belong to family talk and are not considered acceptable outside the home. Be careful to convey the information in a neutral manner, showing no personal distaste for any given words, no matter how you feel about them privately; the idea is not to impose value judgments but to present appropriate substitute expressions. Some children are unaware of the actual meaning of words they use or of substitute words for vulgarisms. By teaching the alternatives, you can help a child become more comfortable with his vocabulary at school without condemning words with which he is more comfortable at home. When discussing the matter, make it clear that all families talk about things that are private, and avoid any suggestion of disapproval of the child's family. This point is important to maintaining the youngster's intrinsic need to respect and trust his own beginnings.

After you talk with the student, ignore all his or her use of inappropriate language (and all peer reactions to it). Rather, seize every occasion to praise him when he expresses himself in conventional terms.

After overhearing Chuck refer to chipped beef on toast served at the school cafeteria as shit on a shingle, Chuck's teacher discovered in private conversation with him that he didn't know the real name of that entree. He quickly accepted the more conventional term and never again used the less acceptable one at school.

It can be argued that deliberately influencing a child to employ different language in different settings is to encourage dishonesty; but this kind of adaptation to varying circumstances represents common courtesy and a normal desire to keep from offending other people. As children mature, they lose their dependence on adults and gain individual freedom of choice, but when they are small they need adult acceptance in order to be free to grow. Teaching a double standard is less likely to impart attitudes of superficial sycophancy than it is to help the youngster understand the realities of his world.

12
GRADES, CHECKLISTS, AND REPORTS

Marks, whether on report cards or tests or papers, are really a way for teachers and parents to judge performance. For a grade to be valuable (to a student) it must be given just after the test is taken. Students rarely bother looking at a test that's returned days or weeks later. Correcting work right then and there is the only way to make sure a student sees his mistakes and learns something from the test.[1]

B. F. SKINNER

1. B. F. Skinner, in an interview with Maria Wilhelm. Reprinted from October 1975 issue of *Family Circle Magazine*, p.183. ©1975 The Family Circle, Inc.

At all levels of education, there is an implied assumption that assignments are given merely to arrive at grades. An assignment is a learning tool. Grades yielded by students who do the assignment measure two things: how much the student has learned and how effectively the teacher has taught. Although every teacher ostensibly knows this, one often hears complaints from teachers about "dumb" or inattentive classes. If you intend to maintain a grading procedure that will keep you informed on instructional points needing review and/or clarification, you'll consistently use grades earned by students to reexamine your own teaching procedures in light of the particular characteristics of each student and individual class. Grades are of little value unless they are used to evaluate the double function of an assignment.

The best time to make full use of such evaluations is immediately after an assignment is done. When a paper is returned several days (or even one day) after it was turned in, the student is apt to glance at it to see his grade, then toss it aside. Most papers can be graded promptly and with student participation, which will serve to hold the attention of both teacher and class on the task that has just been completed. This helps the teacher to clear up points not thoroughly understood and provides opportunities for students to assimilate factual knowledge at a time when these things are still fresh in everyone's mind.

Oral recitations and reports, too, should receive teacher and class comments and suggestions immediately after presentation; if specific standards are set for grades, the class can take part in marking each student's performance. Certainly, this is preferable to having the student return to his seat in silence while the teacher impassively places a snap-judgment evaluation in the grade book. When the latter is practiced, usually only a few students inquire about their grades.

GRADING IN SPECIAL CLASSROOMS

Standard letter or number grading systems have a legitimate place in special education classrooms; however, they should not be used with a child who has been diagnosed emotionally impaired until preparations are begun for screening him into the educational mainstream. Most such youngsters, having experienced discouragement and/or failure in school, tend to react negatively to a standard grade, either ignoring it or placing more importance on the grade itself than on the subject matter being taught. Begin with individual evaluation sheets that list each child's academic subjects and behavioral goals, showing grading values "good," "fair," and "try again," as described and illustrated in chapter 3. Subject grade values can be entered upon completion of each day's work on a subject—either individually or through group discussion, depending on whether or not the whole class is involved. Evaluation of behaviors is usually made at the end of the school day, and students should be included in the evaluation process (see chapter 3).

When grading papers with a student, call his attention to correct responses he has made rather than to his incorrect ones. Mark right answers with an "R" or some other symbol of your choice, leaving wrong answers unmarked for the child to correct after any points he may have misunderstood can be cleared up. Simply telling a child that his efforts have produced a wrong answer, instead of informing him that he must do some more work in order to achieve the right answer, can make a significant difference in his attitude. The second approach is not only less likely to be interpreted as rejection by a student with a history of failure, it also suggests that he is expected to do well—that when his answers are all correct, his task will be completed—and this is conducive to helping him make a persistent effort.

It goes without saying that students' efforts cannot be stimulated by having correct answers furnished. Students who are shown how to test their own answers in math, or how to look up correct answers in any subject after an assignment is done, are stimulated to put forth efforts to reach right answers on their own. As you work with each youngster, you'll be able to recognize the fine line between helping him think for himself and doing his thinking for him. If you have any doubts, it's wise to give more support than you suspect is needed rather than to take the chance of leaving the student floundering in uncertainty. On the other hand, bear in mind that unnecessary help extended consistently can encourage the child toward dependence, as illustrated by the case of Martha (see chapter 9) who learned to make mistakes to receive attention. Through trial-and-error with each individual student, you can learn to sense whether you are expecting the approximate degree of performance the child's ability can reach.

Should a student continue to make errors after attempting to correct his wrong answers, you can let what happens next depend on him. If he slams his book down and refuses to try again with your help, simply ignore this inappropriate reaction. If his negative emotional behavior persists beyond the point where you can ignore it—or if it causes disruption of his classmates' work—calmly isolate the youngster, informing him that he'll be readmitted to the group after he has completed the unfinished assignment. If the class should move on to another activity before he decides to do the work, continue to exclude him, but remain ready to extend further help whenever he exhibits reasonable willingness to tackle the job again. Eventually, he'll come to understand that his reentry to the class is contingent on his own decision to apply further effort to the task at hand.

When a child goes hurriedly over a paper that needs rectifying, guessing at the correct answers (if you know he understands the process for arriving at acceptable answers), you could regain his interest by offering positive clues. For example, you might say, "This problem would have been right if you had remembered to carry only one number," or, "This word would be perfect if you hadn't left out a letter." A child who tends to be careless, impatient, or indifferent is more apt to respond to this kind of assistance, which includes the assumption that his past efforts were not completely wasted; and positive clues often help such children to notice their own errors in the future.

EVALUATION OF
BEHAVIORS

Without exception, check sheets that evaluate behaviors must be tailored to each student's long-term and short-term goals. No checklist fits more than one child, but any checklist is profoundly effective if it fits an individual child and is used properly. Participation of each student in the marking of his daily behavior check sheet becomes a quickly accomplished routine once it is systematized. Students can confer with you privately at your desk and interviews can be kept brief, with the entire process taking place within the last half-hour of the school day. This period could be set aside for free activities devoted to individual interests, with each youngster coming to your desk in turn for check sheet work during the thirty minutes. If token economy is being practiced, those students wishing to spend points they have earned at the class store could do so after their sheets are marked.

Having assisted in the formulation of his goals and being fully aware of whatever consequences he has agreed to, a student usually cooperates readily in making evaluations of his behavior—provided the evaluating is kept on an objective basis. Since each child is aware of his own problem areas, it is appropriate to ask questions such as, "Did you have any trouble with kicking or hitting today?" If he responds negatively, and you actually observed him hitting Tommy, instead of saying, "But I saw you strike Tommy," frame your reminder as a question, "Did you forget the time you struck Tommy?" A child tends to admit his oversight if you remain impassive and concentrate on marking the record accurately. A student who has difficulty admitting to an inappropriate behavior should be sincerely commended for having remembered it following such a prompt; this helps him maintain his self-respect and incidentally encourages him to be more open in the future.

Some children argue at times that your evaluations of their behavior are wrong or unfair. Whenever this occurs, simply review the target behaviors previously agreed on and recorded. When your judgment is based on fact, the child is more apt to accept it. You can end the discussion on a positive note by mentioning that tomorrow will bring new chances to earn a better evaluation.

Occasionally a student makes it a point to tell you of something you failed to notice. You might say, "Well, Susan, you kept from losing your temper all day, didn't you?" and Susan replies, "No—I got mad and pushed James but you didn't see me!" Your proper course of action would be to give strong verbal praise for Susan's truthfulness while duly recording the pushing episode on her check sheet.

REPORTS TO
PARENTS

When sending daily or weekly reports to parents, it's advisable to write down reasons for any evaluation on the report itself, thus allowing no room for doubt in the parents' minds as to your reasons for making the evaluation.

A copy of the same checklist used in the classroom can be sent home with the child. Some parents set up reward systems at home that are contingent on the evaluation sheet, using privileges or tangible reinforcers. Your detailed and careful assistance in setting up and monitoring this kind of parental cooperation can mean an increase (or creation) of positive communication between parent and child; however, as stated in chapter 11, in some families the practice could bring undesirable results, so it should be used with caution.

If a parental contingency system turns out not to be in harmony with the one used at school, check sheets to those parents should be limited to occasions when a personal conference can be used to explain them thoroughly. When parents are overly permissive or indifferent to their child's behavior, check sheets sent home serve no useful purpose. On the other hand, when parents tend to be punitive and judgmental, their child may pretend to lose his check sheet or even to fake a parent's signature on it to avoid showing it at home. Whenever this happens, or when a student tries to influence your marks on his check sheet by telling you that bad evaluations will cause him to be punished severely at home, confine your reports to telephone calls and parent conferences—at least until after you have made further attempts to establish consistency between home contingencies and those used at school.

In the majority of cases, you're able to reach a workable understanding with parents, which greatly benefits the child's progress. The main thing to remember is that parents' confidence in your sincerity, like that of their children, can usually be gained through honest, open discussion.

Laura refused to take an evaluation sheet home because (although she did not disagree with its assessment) it included the reporting of an unacceptable behavior. When she threw the sheet in the wastebasket, the teacher said, "I don't have to depend on that—I can call your mother and tell her directly."

That evening when the mother received the telephone call, she told the teacher that Laura had evidently retrieved the sheet from the wastebasket, since she had brought it home. The teacher encouraged Laura's mother to give the child credit for her willingness to bring the check sheet home despite its unfavorable mark, and to express her confidence that the next day's report would show improvement.

REPORTS FROM PARENTS

Some parents, especially those who notice distinct improvement in their child's self-management after he has been in your room several weeks, will be eager to try out your methods at home. In a conference with them *and their child*, you can explain the checklist system and help them to formulate a check sheet to be marked by them and sent to school each morning via the student.

It's a good idea to keep up a full exchange of information between home and school, if possible. A check sheet marked by parents not only serves as an aid in coordinating home and school efforts to help a child take responsibility, but also tends to make such efforts more consistent.

Target behaviors established for the home situation should be confined, like those fixed for in-school circumstances, to a limited number of principal goals. Success in reaching self-control in one area of behavior usually generalizes to other areas. A daily home check sheet could read something like the following example.

Yes No

1. David hung up his school clothes .... ☐ ☐
2. David came to dinner when called .... ☐ ☐
3. David fed the dog without being reminded .... ☐ ☐
4. David was kind to his sister .... ☐ ☐
5. David was ready for the bus on time .... ☐ ☐

Signed _____ (parent)

Like school check sheets, home check sheets can be mimeographed at school and supplied in quantity. Although preparation of these forms may seem time-consuming, they almost always prove to be worth the extra early effort because they add to everyday organization and consistency. Most parents and their children welcome the substitution of a check sheet, and its specified consequences, for repetitious reminders and nagging in the home.

BUS CHECK SHEETS

As a rule, bus drivers cooperate by marking a short check list on the behaviors of a given special education student, since check sheets assist the driver in keeping order. To acquire the participation of a driver, first explain the advantages of the procedure to him and obtain his agreement to try it; then ask your principal to endorse the agreement.

A check list furnished to a school bus driver should contain no more than one to three main target behaviors and thus, like other behavior check sheets, must be prepared individually. A typical bus check sheet would look like this:

		Yes	No	
1.	Trina remained in her seat at all times	☐	☐	a.m.
		☐	☐	p.m.
2.	Trina talked in a quiet voice	☐	☐	a.m.
		☐	☐	p.m.
3.	Trina refrained from hitting or kicking	☐	☐	a.m.
		☐	☐	p.m.

When the child's parents are working with you, bus behavior check lists can be stapled to each student's school check sheet for the driver to mark and initial when the child leaves the bus in the afternoon, so previously-stipulated consequences of after-school bus behavior can be administered at home. The child returns both sheets the next morning, with the bus driver's before-school evaluations for that day marked and initialed for the teacher.

Children who are not taking check sheets home to their parents would leave their bus check sheets with the driver overnight, for return to the teacher the next morning.

CHECK SHEETS
DURING
PHASING-OUT

Some teachers of special classrooms send daily academic and behavior check sheets for children who are being phased into regular classrooms for one or more subjects to be marked and returned by the regular classroom teacher. Since the practice tends to set the special education student apart from those in the normal classroom, it might serve to detract from the aim of giving him practice at fitting into the educational mainstream. Consequently, any check sheets used should be marked in the special education room, in the presence of the student but not under the observation of his mainstream classmates.

When another teacher takes your entire class for a subject such as physical education, music, or art, you can either ask that teacher to make brief evaluations of behavior on a daily basis or attend each session yourself until you feel confident your students will function adequately without special supervision. One way of encouraging your entire class to demonstrate self-management while with another teacher is to engage in a rap session, to set up target behaviors for that situation, with a highly desired class activity as the reward for meeting certain goals. This sometimes results in the effective control of one or two frequent offenders, through pressures exerted by their classmates.

Essentially, however, the screening out process is an individual one and it requires unique consideration of each student's capacity for growth. It is discussed in the last chapter.

13
TOKEN ECONOMY

That virtue is her own reward, is but a cold principle.

SIR THOMAS BROWNE, *Religio Medici*

"Virtue is her own reward" may be a cold principle, but it expresses a belief that is generally accepted in our society. Persons who take independent responsibility for behaving virtuously are rewarded by freedom from social rejection as well as by the personal satisfaction of being virtuous. However, before one learns to exhibit virtue as a matter of course, he encounters countless experiences involving opportunities to choose between what is right and what is wrong.

Most so-called emotionally impaired children are unaware of their own power to examine such opportunities and to make deliberate decisions concerning them. Such youngsters tend to regard themselves as helpless strugglers in a capricious environment that they can only attempt to control, avoid, or escape through emotionally determined decisions.

You can help each student recognize the difference between right and wrong behaviors, and you can guide him toward conscious choices to utilize behaviors that are socially and academically appropriate for him. Nevertheless, his becoming intellectually aware of his power to control such choices does not automatically bring voluntary substitution of new behaviors for old ones; initially, he requires frequent reminders—a fact he may readily accept in principle, if not always in practice.

An ordinary verbal reminder, delivered as often as it might be necessary in any single case in your classroom, can carry implications of nagging, however pleasantly it is spoken. The practice of skipping reminders and, instead, rewarding (reinforcing) appropriate choices at the instant they are made has proved to be well-tolerated by students and also to be effective in teaching new behaviors. Suggested reinforcers include teacher attention, praise, and the awarding of special privileges.

However, some types of emotional impairment can cause children to react negatively to attention and praise. The severely withdrawn and the overly suspicious are two types of children who may tend to shrink from or ignore sincere verbal expressions of approval. Furthermore, when a teacher is working with up to ten students—each one (at least at the outset) a candidate for almost perpetual reinforcement—comments such as, "That's fine," "You're trying hard," and, "Good job," can lose potency with repetition. Teachers as well as students may lose enthusiasm when kinds of reinforcement are not diversified.

To provide a reinforcement method that can be paired with attention and praise and that offers both variety and tangible evidence of a child's success, many teacher-therapists have adopted some type of token economy. This chapter offers general information about token economy, limiting its application to classrooms for emotionally impaired children, with the aim of providing sufficient knowledge for you to use it. For detailed scientific information on the subject and for in-depth discussions of token economy's role as a *psychological tool,* we refer you to appendix 1, "Suggested Reading for Teachers."

The present chapter is in four sections. This introductory section contains a limited definition of token economy, which describes its use within a context limited to this book and provides some answers to frequently stated criticisms of the system. The second section begins with a general description of techniques to dispense tokens in the classroom, followed by a set of ten rules governing these techniques. Other important aspects of the system, including phasing out tokens after they have served their purpose, are discussed in this section. The third section is concerned with that part of token economy designated as *rewards.* Reasons for using rewards, how to choose them, and general instruction for assigning token values to them will be given. The final section presents a list of hazards for you to consider before adopting token economy in your classroom and a list of advantages the system can provide when used by teacher-therapists.

What Is Token Economy?

When applied in classrooms for emotionally impaired children, token economy is a motivational system employed as follows:

1. Student exhibits a previously agreed-on, clearly stated target behavior that is on his daily check sheet.
2. Teacher-therapist or an assistant exhibits *immediate* positive recognition of the behavior by awarding student a small token reinforcer.
3. Process is repeated as many times as student exhibits the desired behavior, which enables him to accumulate tokens or not, in correspondence to his choice of behavior.
4. At a specified time, student is given the opportunity to exchange tokens he has collected for a more meaningful reward of his own choice.

The purposes of tokens are to provide immediate positive response to the desired behavior; to furnish tangible evidence of the student's use of the behavior; and to bridge the delay between the behavior and delivery of more meaningful rewards.

Tokens can be any small objects: poker chips, plastic counters, paper clips, buttons, paper stars or points noted on a check sheet.

The assignment of values to tokens and rules for their effective use will be discussed under the separate heading, ''Rules for Using Tokens.'' The rewards for which tokens are exchanged can consist of tangibles such as small toys, construction kits, coloring materials, food snacks, and other inexpensive items or intangibles such as free time and other privileges.

The financing, selection, and distribution of rewards will be considered under the separate heading, ''Rewards.''

We made reference to the rationale behind token economy in chapter 3, ''Goals,'' where we pointed out that payment for productive effort is inherent in the general functioning of free enterprise and that mature individuals learn to save their earnings to acquire various rewards. The case related in that chapter involving two brothers who were subject to enuresis, whose mother doled out their allowances in small increments each night they stayed dry, approximated token economy—despite differing in several respects. Before considering rules for use of token economy and surveying its risks and advantages, some frequently encountered general criticisms of the system should be answered.

Answers to Criticisms of Token Economy

Some critics of token economy denounce it as a procedure that employs bribery. This reflects misunderstanding. The American College Dictionary (Random House, 1963) defines the word *bribe* as ''any valuable consideration given or promised for corrupt behavior.'' In the sense in which token economy is used in this chapter, it cannot be described by the word *bribe* because its stated aim is to reward only socially and academically desirable behaviors.

Other critics have alleged that the system employs cold, mechanical techniques by which one human being can insensitively manipulate another human being. From this point of view, token economy might be equated with the bell in Pavlov's laboratory that activated the hunger reflex in that pioneer behaviorist's drooling experimental canines. Unfortunately, attitudes and terminology commonly used by some proponents of behavior modification (the modern discipline that developed token economy) may have inadvertently contributed to this impression.

There is no question that token economy—or any other system for influencing behavior—can be misused by indifferent or unscrupulous persons. Conventional behavior-shaping methods, which rely on arbitrarily stated rules, coercion and punishment, have succeeded for centuries in guiding most people along lines of social conformity. Obviously these methods, too, can be used either with compassion and respect for human dignity or with coldness and indifference to the feelings of others.

A philosophy of teaching that endorses the democratic classroom supports any disciplinary method—regardless of its label—provided that method recognizes individual differences, human rights, and workable learning principles. Token economy, which promises a clearly understood reward for specific desired behavior, is no more manipulative than a system that promises retribution following undesired behavior. Furthermore, token economy often succeeds in guiding emotionally impaired children to growth in self-management after conventional methods have failed.

Since token economy is rapidly becoming an accepted tool in special education, you may be required to use it in the school system that employs you. Whether or not the choice is left to you, it is recommended that you become acquainted with its procedures, because the principles of token economy, as interpreted in this chapter, bring to a focus the disciplinary philosophy presented in all other chapters of this book.

TOKENS
General Classroom Procedures

Consider the token-awarding procedures used in classrooms under the School Adjustment Program, a countywide plan involving special education of emotionally impaired children in the Kalamazoo Valley Intermediate School District, Kalamazoo, Michigan. Here is a description.

A token economy is employed in every School Adjustment Program classroom, with poker chips serving as tokens. . . . We give tokens immediately, while the behavior is occurring, as well as at fixed intervals, because we conceive of the tokens primarily as reinforcers for desirable operant behavior rather than as positive events that reduce the child's negative emotional reactions to school and learning (though they may do this as well). In addition, we dispense tokens for a much wider variety of behaviors, depending on our behavioral objectives for the child and for the group. For example, tokens have been used to reward a profoundly withdrawn child for knocking the teacher's books off her desk (an assignment given to teach greater assertiveness), to reward another isolate child for initiating social interaction . . . to reward a complainer for beginning a task without complaint, to reward a boy who had stolen tokens for going a prescribed period of time (we began with a thirty-minute criterion) without stealing, to reward a very shy boy for requesting help rather than crying when he had difficulty on an academic task, and to reward many children for such behaviors as reading expressively, working quietly, reading a line without error, participating in discussion, or ignoring a classmate who is being noisy.

Tokens are used liberally and are often paired with praise, pats on the back, or other social reinforcers. The tokens are dropped in small containers on the children's desks. This produces a sound that makes it unnecessary for the child to even look up momentarily to detect the receipt of a token, and we find it is not disruptive to the child after his first hour or two in the classroom.[1]

This overview illustrates how token reinforcers are dispensed; the rules for using tokens[2] that follow elaborate on that procedure. The subject of rewards that can be purchased with tokens accumulated by each student is discussed in the next section.

Rules for Using Tokens

1. Exact agreement: State each target behavior exactly, in simple language the child can understand and agree with, and clearly define the value of the token that will be used to reward it. Since this point has been covered repeatedly, the reason for the rule—to eliminate subjective judgment from the reinforcement process—needs no elaboration.

2. Direct supervision: Furnish direct, systematic supervision of each youngster. Even with the help of one or more assistants, you cannot be expected to provide continuous supervision of each child in your class; however, supervision can be maximized by not following a set pattern or routine that would make it easily predictable. Frequent but irregular intervals of supervision are preferable to constant supervision, because they tend to keep a student alert while simultaneously allowing intervals of independence, which become longer as he progresses toward his self-management goals.

3. One supervisor at a time: During any given period of supervision, assign one—and only one—individual to supervise and dispense reinforcers to each student. The practical reason for this rule was exemplified in the chapter 9 report on Martha, the word-caller whose performance regressed after a supervisor unknowingly reinforced her errors. When primary responsibility for each child's reinforcement procedure is given a single supervisor, possible errors in supervision can be isolated and corrected more easily than when more than one supervisor is involved.

Other reasons for this rule are that individual supervisors tend to establish better rapport in specific activities with certain children, and a single supervisor's repeated contacts with a child can yield increased general understanding of the child's idiosyncracies.

4. Share all records: Keep all supervisors abreast of each student's status. It's obvious that placing each child under permanently exclusive supervision by one person would not be feasible. It's necessary that you and your helpers share knowledge of each student's academic level, behavioral goals and current level of progress, so supervisory duties for any

1. Robert P. Hawkins, "The School Adjustment Program: Individualized Intervention for Children with Behavior Disorders," Kalamazoo Valley Intermediate School District. Paper presented at Second Annual Kansas Symposium on Behavior Analysis in Education, Lawrence, Kans., May 1971.
2. Most of these rules were restated for application to elementary special education classrooms from *The Token Economy*, Teodoro Ayllon and Nathan Azrin, Century Psychology Series (New York: Meredith Corporation, Appleton-Century-Croft, 1968).

one activity can be transferred in cases of absences and other unexpected interruptions of routines. Furthermore, it's advisable to rotate all supervision so each adult works with each child in at least one area daily, to provide students with variety and to broaden their interpersonal relationships.

5. Accuracy: Dispense tokens accurately. This rule is made easy to follow by observance of the preceding rules. When the target behavior is precisely understood and its token values are fixed, an alert supervisor can maintain maximum fairness and accuracy in awarding (or withholding) tokens.

6. Promptness: Dispense tokens promptly. Award each token as the desired behavior occurs or as soon as possible afterward. The importance of immediate feedback cannot be overstated, since each token symbolizes recognition of a successful performance. Immediate feedback also contributes to consistency and accuracy on the part of the supervisor.

7. Bridge necessary delay: When a token cannot be immediately awarded, signal the child who has earned it. During times when your attention must be divided between several students, occasional delays in dispensing tokens become necessary. At such times, notify children of your intention to award tokens they have coming to them, either verbally or with smiles, nods, or gestures.

A second kind of necessary delay must be made when a student who has just earned a token engages in an unacceptable behavior (either related or unrelated to the one being reinforced) before the token can be delivered.

Mary raised her hand instead of shouting the answer to a question the teacher had asked the class; but before the teacher's aide could reinforce her, Mary poked the child at the desk in front of her with a ruler. The aide withheld reinforcement until after the incident involving the ruler had been discussed with Mary; only then did the student receive praise and the token she had earned by raising her hand.

8. Incremental behaviors: Reinforce behaviors that seem to initiate, or to move the student in the direction of, his target behavior.

One of Bill's target behaviors was to use his handkerchief instead of allowing his nose to run. When Bill's nose began to run, rather than reminding him, the teacher issued a combination of verbal and token reinforcement the instant Bill's hand moved in the general direction of his handkerchief.

9. Vary the reinforcers: Use many different kinds of tokens. Poker chips make excellent all-purpose tokens. Their three colors represent point values that correspond to the decimal system and to monetary ex-

change at simple levels, which facilitates transfer of knowledge to arithmetic concepts and money transactions. However, individual target behaviors should be reinforced with a large variety of kinds of tokens; this is covered under rule ten, specialization of reinforcers.

Varying the shapes, sizes, textures, and colors of tokens will enable you to avoid the phenomenon token economists call *satiation,* which denotes a youngster's loss of interest due to overuse of a single reinforcer. A change in type of token is also of use in verifying a child's progress from one step to another.

10. Specialization of reinforcers: Assign individual token systems to some children. This rule serves to individualize token economy in the classroom, as it allows the establishment of a reinforcement system commensurate with the child's unique situation. To begin with, choose one standard all-purpose token that has an identical value for the entire class. This token is the one to be accumulated by students for purchase of rewards and special privileges. As the need for dividing target behaviors into incremental steps becomes less, specialized tokens can be dropped and the standard token can be awarded for most target behaviors.

The main reason poker chips make good standard tokens is that they provide a basic rate of exchange. From the first day of school, they can be used for individual reinforcement of general class rules (settling down to work within five minutes after the bell; returning from recess on time). At the same time, they can be used in their various denominations for reinforcing individual target behaviors; and, also at the same time, point values represented by the standard chips can be subdivided *for each child* through use of special reinforcers dispensed in response to his incremental behaviors.

Specialization of reinforcers can be best explained by illustration. The following chart shows how the system can be applied to a single target behavior, in relation to three different students.

Child's Name	Target Behavior	Unit of Measurement	Token	Exchange Rate
April	remain quiet during work	1 minute	1 button	5 buttons = 1 white chip
Pete	appropriate bathroom behavior	each visit to bathroom	1 gold star	2 stars = 1 red chip
Tammy	learn multiplication tables	1 correct answer	1 paper clip	2 paper clips = 1 white chip

Thus, you can see that specialization of reinforcers can enable a teacher to place weights on various tokens in correspondence to each student's unique characteristics.

Another way to specialize a reinforcer is to set up a completely individualized system that bears no relationship either to the standard token or to rewards earned by the rest of the class. Used effectively to eliminate severely incapacitating or self-mutilating habits, this kind of specialization is used with one child exclusively. A distinctive token, not available to any other student, is used; and rewards consist of prizes and/or privileges especially coveted by the individual youngster. The case of Connie, whose habit of eye-poking was eliminated through this method, is related under the next heading, fines.

Fines

If your class should decide to establish a penalty plan at the time class rules are being made, exact penalties must be written into the rules. Besides specifying deprivation of certain privileges for some offenses, if token economy is being used a limited number (two or three at most) of serious rule-infringements could be designated to require token fines. Like the dispensing of tokens, the charging of fines must be consistent with recorded agreement and promptly executed in direct response to infringement of rules definitely associated with fines. Of course, a new student in the room would be exempt from all penalties until after he has become familiar with the class rules.

Fines can also be used on an individual basis, by withdrawing tokens previously earned through an appropriate behavior on occurrence of its opposite inappropriate behavior. Again, such fines must be fixed on mutual agreement and assigned to specific acts that are opposite counterparts of target behaviors.

Use of fines with individual students is not recommended except to bring to conscious attention deeply ingrained, frequently practiced habits that have become so automatic as to require persistent prompting. Mumbling, thumb sucking, squinting, masturbating, and nail biting are habits in this category. Tics, gestures, facial contortions, and other unconscious behaviors typically seen to accompany physical impairment can also be reduced or eliminated by alternating the delivery of reinforcers for controlling such habits with the repossession of reinforcers after lapses in control.

Connie, a congenitally blind twelve-year-old, was habituated to eye-poking, one of the characteristic habits associated with sightlessness called blindisms. *Eye-poking results from obsessive preoccupation with the eyes and is marked by incessant pushing at the eyeballs with fingers, fists, or objects. The habit attracted undesirable attention to Connie and was so persistent that it was threatening to force her eyeballs behind their sockets, thus damaging the child's attractive facial appearance.*

A project to eliminate the habit was set up in the schoolroom. An empty plastic margarine container was taped to the right side of Connie's desk; another container, filled with plastic bingo markers, was taped to the left side of the desk. Between nine a.m. and noon daily, the child was observed at random intervals. If she was not engaged in eye-poking, she was praised and told to take a chip from the dish on the left and place it in the one on the right. Weekly goals were set in percentages of times Connie was observed to be refraining from the habit, with the daily percentage being recorded on a master sheet. When the target percentage was met during a given week, Connie could exchange the chips she had earned for phonograph records, outings, desired articles of clothing, and other rewards, most of them furnished by her parents. During this phase of the project, eye-poking dropped from the baseline condition of about 85 percent to an average of 60 percent of the time.

In the second phase, a plan involving fines was used. In addition to being rewarded for meeting reasonable goals for elimination of eye-poking, Connie was expected to surrender chips she had previously earned when goals were not met. Whenever she engaged in eye-poking, she took a chip from the dish on her right and returned it to the dish on her left. Connie's eye-poking dropped to virtually zero during the first week after fines were instituted.[3]

Phasing Out of Tokens

It has been emphasized that the use of token economy closely corresponds to a child's rate of academic and social growth. Assuming that each student understands his target behaviors and long-term goals and that he is regularly consulted for updating on his progress, one of his ultimate objectives should be to abandon a highly structured incentive system for encouragement of normally expected behaviors. Since return to a regular classroom represents final evidence that he has outgrown the need for unusual amounts of reinforcement for appropriate behaviors, phasing out of tokens should go hand in hand with his gradual achievement of self-management.

The following abstract is taken from a case reported by one of the authors and her student assistant at the time of the study.

Near the end of his phasing-out process, when he was taking most of his classes in a regular fifth-grade room but was still based in the special classroom, John announced that he wished to become accustomed to working without tokens. "There won't be tokens at my old school when I

3. Unpublished study by Duane L. Trombly and Doris B. Mosier, 1974.

*go back," he explained, "and I'll soon be in junior high—I'm getting too
big for that kind of stuff."*

*His supervisors praised John for his mature decision and
congratulated him further when he refused to accept the tokens he
had earned that day. His classmates expressed admiration (although not
one of them indicated desire to emulate him); one boy said, "Some day
I'll be like John—then I can go back to my old school."*

*John was made permanent manager and record keeper of the class
store, with a salary consisting of check points which he saved for weekly
purchases at the store. On being screened out of the special classroom,
John was honored at a maturity party, hosted by the special room and
attended by his friends in the class he was about to enter.*[4]

REWARDS

In most cities, there's at least one shop where money has no purchasing
power. This shop is crammed full of merchandise with prices marked not
in dollars and cents but in quantities of trading stamps. A trading stamp in
itself is essentially worthless. However, people who collect books full of
trading stamps can exchange them at a trading stamp outlet for valuable
merchandise; thus they are participating in a process that in many ways
resembles token economy. The comparison holds, however, only to the
door of the shop offering trading stamp merchandise—because rewards
offered there are priced in stamp quantities that are based on actual
monetary worth.

In token economy, token values placed on rewards are related to group
popularity rather than to real currency values. An inexpensive puzzle, if
highly desired by most of your students, might be priced at 300 tokens; an
extremely nutritious snack worth twice as much as the puzzle might be
priced at only 50 points. In the same way, corn chips, candy bars, and
frivolous toys might cost more token points than structured learning materials such as flash cards.

Stocking the Class
Store

The class store is financed by your room's miscellaneous expense
allowance from the school district. Care in selection of rewards can
extend a limited amount of money to purchase of a large variety of
inexpensive items enjoyed by youngsters. Choice of rewards that appeal
to your students varies from one year to another, depending on individual
and group preferences. A child who is interested in animals should be
given the opportunity to save tokens for small books about animals, and
children who like games should find games on display at the class store.

Privileges as
Rewards

Highly desired activities and certain class responsibilities can be used
as rewards. Ten minutes of free time to work on art or another preferred

4. Doris Mosier and Joseph J. Vaal, Jr., "Dependency on Material Reinforcers," *School Applications of Learning Theory,* Kalamazoo Valley Intermediate School District 3, No. 3 (April 1971), p. 13.

activity could be priced at a specific number of tokens. Library privileges, a turn at changing the calendar, and various other jobs children might ask to do would be valued according to their relative popularity and importance.

All daily jobs should be rotated. The only time it is advisable to give one student a regular or permanent job would be when the student has progressed beyond the use of tokens, and in such a case the job itself would be compensated by points for that student's use in acquiring rewards of his choice. One coveted privilege is that of dispensing tokens to other students. If you allow it at all, this job should be considered a very special one, in reward for extraordinary achievement; and the student engaged in it must be fully supervised. Allowing a student to dispense tokens can help him understand the teacher's job, lend insight into his own behaviors, and provide experience in use of fair, objective judgment.

Sampling Rewards

To ensure variety of reward items and also to help broaden students' experiences, new articles should be placed in the store each time the stock is replenished. However, before offering new rewards for sale, make sure your students are given chances to develop eagerness to acquire them. Youngsters who have never played with jacks will have no desire to own jacks until they have learned the game; the same is true of anything that can become a coveted reward once its usefulness becomes evident. The practice of sampling rewards is a necessary step in token economy and it should be extended to all newly introduced rewards, including free time activities and library privileges.

Store Time

The most convenient time to open the class store is during the last half-hour of the school day, which coincides with check-sheet evaluation time. After his daily brief conference with the teacher and the marking of his check sheet, each student is entitled to decide what to do with tokens he has earned. He may spend each day's tokens as they are accumulated; he may browse at the store to select a prized item that will require more than a day's earnings; or he may decide to set aside all or part of his tokens each day in a bank account intended for an especially expensive reward.

By broadening options for the use of tokens, you can extend the principle of controlled freedom (discussed in chapter 4) to the entire class, while giving your more mature pupils opportunities to save tokens for delayed, strongly coveted rewards.

Setting Up an Economy

Token prices assigned to rewards must be determined by the relative liberality (or parsimony) of token-distribution. Obviously, when tokens are dispensed generously the economy becomes inflated and prices of rewards must be kept consistently high to prevent their becoming too easily acquired (not to mention resultant depletion of the class budget). Conversely, when too few tokens are put into circulation, it becomes difficult to price rewards low enough to make them purchasable. Ulti-mately, balanced token economy is achieved through trial and error. Fortunately, the process is simpler than it may appear to one who is inexperienced in it—and mistakes are not likely to be catastrophic.

Some examples of token distribution rates were given in the section devoted to tokens. Rates are, of course, based on individual target be-haviors and their probable frequency of occurrence. Once you start work-ing with each student, you'll be able to estimate how many tokens he can earn in a day; from that estimate you can determine reasonable prices for the kinds of rewards he is likely to wish to earn in that time.

In fairness to each student, aim to give every child an equal number of opportunities to earn a given number of standard tokens during the course of a day. Then you should be able to apply the same reward-pricing procedure to the entire class, setting prices according to popular demand as described earlier.

Rewarding
Phase-Out Students

The right to purchase rewards at the class store should be extended to every student for as long as he remains a member of the special class—even though he may be so near the end of his phasing-out practice that he no longer earns tokens for specific appropriate behaviors. The termination of such a youngster's opportunities to claim rewards would clearly amount to penalizing him for having outgrown his need for token reinforcers.

Under the discussion of token phase-out, it was related that one student was given the job of managing the class store after he ceased to receive tokens, with a salary paid in check-points that he could exchange at standard token value. Any regular responsibility can be given job status for assignment in this manner to a student who no longer needs immediate reinforcement of each appropriate behavior. The job becomes a general, prestige-related reward for satisfactory overall daily performance and it enables the child to continue as a class member with eligibility to pur-chase rewards.

RISKS AND
ADVANTAGES
OF TOKEN ECONOMY

Information about applications of token economy in classes for emo-tionally impaired children would be incomplete without some words of caution concerning problems that can be encountered in using the system and a final summing up of advantages that can be realized when its techniques are utilized fairly and democratically. This section of the chapter is intended partially as a review of what has been presented. Its main purpose, however, is to provide opportunities for you to consider whether you wish to establish a token economy in your classroom.

Risks in Using Token
Economy

A casual observer of token economy in operation might conclude that it is a simple, easily administered system that works quite automatically. This apparent simplicity probably represents the method's most serious hazard. Like any other system used to motivate specific aspects of social and academic growth, token economy demands alertness against carelessness in its practice. Careless use of any system can result in failure; and if token economy is to accomplish its purposes, those who use it need to know its risks and to guard against them.

The following list names principal risks to be avoided when using token economy. Being aware of these risks should help you maintain vigilance for a variety of similar or related pitfalls that might develop within your own unique set of circumstances.

1. Techniques can become automatic. A teacher who walks around the classroom dispensing tokens indiscriminately, without paying careful attention to whether they have been earned, destroys the usefulness of token economy. The reason for awarding each token should be plainly understood, both by the teacher and the student, or its value may be reduced— sometimes even negated.

2. Tokens can be awarded too liberally. Handing out tokens for a child's every acceptable word and act creates a kind of inflation that cheapens the token and robs the child of any sense of accomplishment. Tokens must be earned through conscious effort and distributed in uniformity with each child's progress toward his established target behaviors.

3. Tokens can be awarded too frugally. Frugal use of tokens can occur when a teacher fails to reinforce incremental behaviors that are related to target behaviors. It may also result from arbitrary or literal interpretations of rules and agreements in such a way that no deviation from verbatim definition is recognized. Such inflexibility is seen in cold, mechanical attitudes, which can stunt the effectiveness of any behavior-shaping method.

One of the rules for room cleanup at a private school was to empty wastebaskets. The teacher in charge of room inspection issued a demerit against Jack because, after emptying his wastebasket, he had dropped a single scrap of paper in it.

Under a token economy system the same teacher probably would have withheld a token because Jack's wastebasket, although it had been emptied, was not literally empty.

4. Techniques can become manipulative. A teacher who yields to emotional pleas for tokens that have not been earned is vulnerable to manipulation by students. On the same note, a teacher who cannot resist using repeated prompts—such as, "If you finish [or don't finish] your problems, you will [or won't] get a token"—is manipulating instead of allowing the child to choose the consequence according to prearranged agreement.

5. Token economy can make children mercenary. After first learning

that certain behaviors earn tokens, some children use such behaviors excessively or resort to pretense "while teacher is looking" to collect tokens. To counteract such practices, careful observation of each student is necessary until he learns to comprehend the distinction between superficial game playing and actualization that makes a behavior meaningful in terms of social and/or academic results.

6. Token economy can make children dependent on reinforcement for normally expected behaviors. This hazard can be mitigated by careful adherence to procedures that keep each child an active participant throughout his special education program. A student who consciously recognizes the cause or causes for his being placed in your room, assists in setting his own goals, and knows that attaining those goals will result in progress toward return to a normal classroom is not likely to become over dependent on token economy.

Nevertheless, the risk exists in a few cases in which a child clings to the security offered by a highly structured disciplinary system by refusing to accept responsibilities that offer him greater freedom. Sometimes transfer of the child to another classroom for emotionally impaired students at a higher grade level serves to stimulate him to grow up.

7. Token economy can be used unnecessarily. Just as a youngster who is learning to balance his body should be given only enough physical support to prevent his falling, so should a student who is learning to cope with his emotional difficulties be supported by the minimum necessary environmental structure. A child with problems sufficiently severe to bring a diagnosis of emotional impairment undoubtedly benefits from a behavior-management program more structured than that found in the average classroom; however, not all such children require an equal amount of structure. Care must be taken not to overreinforce any appropriate behavior; in addition, it is vital that reinforcement be gradually reduced as each student grows to exhibit increased self-management ability.

8. Token economy can be applied too generally. Although a child may exhibit a vast array of inappropriate behaviors, only a limited number of priority-based target behaviors should be selected for reinforcement by token economy. Obviously, an individual program involving dozens of goals would be confusing and unwieldy. Furthermore, progress in eliminating one severely debilitating behavior can often influence a child to initiate his own improvement in other behavioral areas.

Advantages of Token Economy

Since comments on the usefulness of a token economy in classrooms for emotionally impaired children have recurred regularly throughout past chapters, the following enumeration of advantages offered by such a system offers only a brief summary.

1. Token economy provides immediate, tangible consequences for student behavior. Through it, students are kept aware of their target behaviors and are able to measure their own progress.

2. It furnishes a method to reinforce students who do not respond positively to praise and other social attention. Children who avoid interpersonal interactions, whether they are withdrawn or suspicious and cynical, often respond to token reinforcers that are not paired with verbal reinforcement.

3. It helps maintain consistency. When used with clearly defined goals and a uniform system of point values, token economy can enhance consistency in dealing with students.

4. It can help keep supervisors on their toes. The method aids teachers and other classroom supervisors in keeping constantly aware of each student's target behaviors and academic goals. It also sustains alertness to each child's current status.

5. It furnishes results that parents can see. The earning of tangible rewards gives a student something he can take home and show to his family as daily (or frequent) proof of his progress. This adds reinforcement to the child and in some cases wins greater parent cooperation.

6. It teaches counting and money skills. Counting tokens and exchanging various values sets the stage for teaching currency values and making change with money.

7. It helps teach math. Use of savings accounts teaches arithmetic processes of addition and subtraction. This also helps a child to learn prudent handling of money as well as patience to save up for a desired goal.

8. It can help students learn judgment. If helping the teacher dispense tokens is made a special privilege a student can earn, this activity gives the child practice in exercising judgment as to whether a reward should or should not be given and—more important—helps him to understand how his own behavior is evaluated.

9. It teaches self-discipline. Proper use of token economy ensures that its use will be phased out as new behaviors replace old, undesirable ones. This is accomplished by periodic revision of target behaviors and consequences, with the student's full knowledge and agreement. A final highly coveted award marks the student's acceptance of independent responsibility for his own actions and accomplishments.

14
PHASING OUT AND SCREENING OUT

When he looked down, what was it that he saw in the water! He was no longer gray and ugly; he was a beautiful swan, with shining feathers as white as snow!

. . . but he was not proud. He remembered how he had been laughed at and poked and bitten. . . . "When I was the ugly duckling," he said, "I did not dream that I could ever be so happy!"

HANS CHRISTIAN ANDERSEN, *The Ugly Duckling*

You cannot expect exposure to your classroom's special environment to effect the eventual transformation of all your emotionally impaired students into consummately "normal" individuals. Nevertheless, given understanding, respect, and consistent treatment, most of your students will show measurable monthly improvement; and you can anticipate sending approximately one-fourth of them back to regular education during the course of each year, with length of time required to screen out individuals varying from one child to another. This 25 percent average is taken from a 1973 study of a countywide program for emotionally impaired children, which involved ninety-six students (average age ten years, five months) whose mean length of time spent in the program was 13.4 months, with a range of 1 to 52 months.[1]

Screening out is the formal, official act of terminating a student's enrollment in special education and reenrolling him in regular education, after the goals established for him have been satisfactorily achieved. While he is working toward those long-term goals through a series of incremental short-term goals, the student can derive great benefit from being given every possible chance to practice newly acquired behaviors in settings outside the special classroom. For this reason, it's advisable that your students be exposed to the routines of regular classes, beginning as soon as they show readiness and continuing for gradually increased periods of time until they can function in regular classrooms under ordinary supervision. The use of phasing out practice depends first of all on each child's rate of development in your room; then it depends on cooperation from your school's administrators and your teaching colleagues.

PHASING OUT
BEGINS ON DAY ONE

Since his re-enrollment within the mainstream of education is the ultimate goal of every special-education student, the process of phasing him or her out of your program should begin on the day the child enters your classroom. The formulation of long-term goals is discussed in chapter 3,

1. Thomas I. Shikoski, Robert P. Hawkins, and Bradley E. Huitema, "Objective Evaluation of a Treatment Program for Severely Maladjusted Children," a paper presented at the Fifth Banff International Conference of Behavior Modification, March 1973.

which additionally explains the uses of short-term goals as incremental steps for reaching the ultimate goals. There, also, the necessity for using written objectives as constant standards for measurement of each child's progress is emphasized.

Even while you are getting to know your students and helping them to become acclimated to their new class, ideally you can already be stimulating them toward kinds of self-management that will eventually enable them to leave that class. During the time they are with you, this thought must be kept uppermost in your mind: your main function is to guide each student toward assuming responsible independence. This is the point on which your professional validity as a teacher-therapist rests; your strength lies in your ability to become concerned about a child, sensitive to his needs—indeed, to some extent, involved in his conflicts—while cooperating with his right to grow beyond all need of you. It demands steadfast watchfulness against the temptation to hold a student in your room beyond the time your records show him ready to move on because of an egotistical assumption that the world will undo the gains he has made in the environment you have provided.

USE OF
INCREMENTAL STEPS
IN PHASING OUT

One technique that can prove helpful to both you and the student is the arrangement of phasing out on an incremental, step-by-step basis. Just as all other long-term goals are approached by gradual steps that involve practicing socially desirable behaviors, the phasing-out process can be practiced by incremental stages, with the cooperation of your colleagues in conventional classrooms. You'll find most other teachers willing to work with you, particularly if you offer them services in return. Some suggestions for reciprocal arrangements will be made further on in this chapter.

As soon as possible after a student enters your classroom, make arrangements to channel him into the mainstream for some portion of his in-school time. Watch each child for indications of special interest— preference for activities such as art, music, or physical education—or high stability and achievement in a certain school subject. Depending on the youngster's progress with behavioral objectives and on your judgment as to his capacity for tolerating conventional school conditions without regression, make arrangements with a teacher of the child's favorite subject (at the appropriate grade level) for your student to attend the regular class. You might begin this as an experiment for as short a time as fifteen minutes per week or per class day, then gradually lengthen the period as the student proves capable of making the adjustment. Until such time that he exhibits sufficient independence to attend the other class on his own, either you or an aide should accompany him and stay in the room— another crutch that can be phased out by degrees.

If the student meets reasonable standards of social and academic success in his practice room, his periods there can be lengthened and finally extended to full-time participation in that one class. Subsequently, as rapidly as the child shows readiness for further phasing-out sessions in other subjects, the process can be repeated until you consider all his long-term goals to have been met.

Before phasing-out procedures are begun, three conditions must be met.

PREREQUISITES TO
PRACTICE PHASING
OUT

1. Full understanding is necessary between the special classroom teacher and other staff members who may become involved on a part-time basis. Ask your school's principal to allow time during a staff meeting to explain the phasing-out process, stressing the importance of practice periods prior to each student's return to regular classes. Emphasize your willingness to reciprocate for instruction given your students. Make it clear that you never expect another teacher to accept a child on more than a part-time basis, and then only when he conforms to the rules of the regular classroom.

In some schools, art, music, and physical education teachers are expected to teach special-education students. This is usually done in separate classes, with the help of an aide or student teacher from the special classroom. When one of your students is ready for practice time in a regular class, however, you might exchange part-time assistance (or the services of one of your helpers) in some capacity designated by the other teacher.

Exchange services in academic subjects could be arranged by your taking the class in which your student is participating, in either your room or the other teacher's, for a given number of lessons. When taking over another teacher's work in that teacher's classroom, be sure to use his or her teaching materials and to stay within the structure of lesson plans already being utilized. On occasions that you receive students from another room for lessons for your class, you can, of course, adhere to your own procedures (assuming that the subject matter covers legally required content for the grade level).

A colleague who consults you on some problem concerning class discipline or an individual student's behavior might be especially amenable to working with your practice students, since the act of seeking your opinion would indicate an interest in your methods. It would *not* be appropriate, however, for you to volunteer consultation services, either in exchange for help with your students nor at any other time. Even when you feel certain that another teacher would profit by suggestions from you, it's imperative that you maintain tacit respect for techniques that differ from your own. Being in charge of the class that has been labeled emotionally impaired may place you in an inferior position rather than in one of authority in the minds of some other faculty members. Consequently, you're wise to solicit the cooperation of your colleagues and quietly allow your own methods to be justified by their results.

2. The student must desire phasing-out practice. The chance to return to a regular classroom should be held up as a privilege to be earned. Each child screened into your room is aware that he has been placed there for certain reasons. In your early contacts with him, the acceptable behavioral goals that you and he list together clarify those reasons in his mind. When you offer him an opportunity to prove his acceptable behaviors in a conventional classroom setting, you endorse the gains he has shown; but if the opportunity comes before he is ready for it, he may not consider it to be a privilege. In any event, allowing him too much time to feel at home in a special room can result in the defeat of his ultimate goal. Thus, aside from all the praise and encouragement he receives for meeting incremental goals within the special setting, chances to participate in regular education—even on a temporary practice basis—must become the supreme reward that he strives for. This was exemplified by the case of John in chapter 13.

Occasionally a child who seems to be ready and appears eager to begin practicing participation in a regular class reverts to previous behaviors. This brings us to the third condition that must be clarified before screening-out practice is undertaken.

3. Until final screening out takes place, the special education room will remain home base for the student. So long as a child remains under your jurisdiction, he must report to your room every morning and continue to spend most of his time with your class. All practice periods in other rooms are strictly on a trial basis, and the student's daily schedule is structured according to well-defined rules. He knows in advance that return to his home room will follow automatically if he fails to maintain appropriate behaviors in his practice room. He is never free to shuttle back and forth from one room to the other at will, but must follow the agreement set up between the two teachers and himself. Neither can deprivation of practice periods be at the caprice of either teacher; it must be based on the terms of the agreement. This calls for complete understanding at the outset between you and the other teacher.

On rare occasions, despite showing both readiness and enthusiasm for practice at phasing out, a child demonstrates continued dependence on the special education room by regressing to his previous inappropriate behaviors, hoping to be returned to home base. You must not tolerate such patent manipulation by a student, but the problem is difficult to solve.

Curtis had learned to use acceptable behaviors at all times in the special classroom and welcomed an opportunity to attend a regular classroom for screening-out practice. Soon after his practice periods began, he reverted to former behaviors while in the new room. He became boisterous and so bellicose that the regular teacher, after many attempts to help him adjust, gave up on keeping him unless his behavior improved.

In conferences with the principal and both of his teachers, Curtis agreed that he could not stay in a special classroom forever and insisted that he liked the new room; but further trial sessions there brought more negative results.

Finally, after it became plain that Curtis would not accept being screened out of the special classroom, he was transferred to another special classroom at a higher grade level.

There are also cases in which emotional problems, although not severe enough to cause institutionalization, never become sufficiently alleviated to make final screening out possible. Most children in this category function acceptably within the structure of a special classroom but persist—there or in any other environment—in displaying deviant behaviors from time to time. You may be able to pinpoint the causes for the inability of some of these recidivists to fully understand and cope with their difficulties, but be powerless to remove those causes—which could be anything from minor brain trauma to an overwhelmingly unhappy home situation. Your only course is to retain such children in your room until they are academically prepared for promotion to a special class at a higher age level.

THE FINAL PHASE: SCREENING OUT

After a student has proved capable of spending full school days in regular classrooms for a period of two to four months, depending on his individual rate of growth, he can be considered ready to return permanently to the educational mainstream. Frequent communication between you and the regular teacher throughout the practice period is essential. Student conferences and also parent conferences should include both teachers, and when the child has been phased into the new room full-time, the regular teacher handles grading and other contacts with parents. During this transition period, the teacher providing transition services plays a highly significant role that enables you to enter the last stages of relinquishing your responsibility.

Meanwhile, you meet with your classroom consultant, the social worker, and/or other school personnel in the childen's home district to consider his permanent placement. After receiving recommendations concerning one or more classrooms, you visit the proposed room or rooms, talk to teachers and principals, and prepare your own final suggestions for the student's permanent placement.

A child with a history of only mild behavioral problems can usually be returned to his former school building—sometimes, if circumstances are favorable, to the same room from which he was referred to special education. A student whose reputation for totally unacceptable classroom behavior is still widespread in his previous school should, if possible, be given a fresh start in new surroundings. When the child's previous school is the only one in his home district, it is advisable that he at least be placed with a different teacher, unless there is no alternative. In any event, the home district teacher must be fully informed regarding the student and his current success in meeting his problems.

Procedures for transferring a child from special education to regular education follow your state's guidelines. Whatever those procedures are, you should do all you can to make the screening-out process a gratifying experience for the child. In some special education rooms a short celebration honoring each student on his last day lends finality to his graduation.

FOLLOW-UP

Most receiving teachers are extremely cooperative in reporting a child's progress during early weeks. If you furnish mimeographed sheets that list behaviors they can check, along with stamped, self-addressed envelopes, a receiving teacher finds it convenient to provide you with follow-up information until adjustments are made. On your part, you can ask the receiving teacher to let you know *immediately* should the student begin to exhibit problem behavior, so that either you or your consultant can offer assistance.

Some students never look back after leaving your classroom. Once finally screened out, these youngsters do not wish to be reminded of their experiences in special education. Other children want to keep in touch with you and their former classmates, sometimes for years after leaving you. It's most advisable that you not instigate extended relationships with former pupils. Let a few weeks go by before you respond to letters; if telephoned, remain friendly but take every opportunity to extol each student's independence in new surroundings. Welcome personal visits warmly, but encourage past students to discuss their problems with their current teachers and counselors. If necessary, remind them of the goals you originally set together—and rejoice with them that those goals were reached.

Appendix 1
Suggested Reading for Teachers

1. BECKER, WESLEY C.; ENGELMANN, SIEGFRIED; AND THOMAS, DON R. *Cognitive Learning and Instruction* (Chicago: Science Research Associates, 1975). *Teaching 1:* Classroom Management; *Teaching 2:* Cognitive Learning and Instruction; *Teaching 3:* Evaluation.

2. DANIELS, LLOYD K., ed. *Management of Child Behavior Problems at School and at Home* (Springfield, Ill.: Charles C. Thomas, 1974).

3. FUKARI, SHIRO. *How Can I Make What I Cannot See?* (New York: Van Nostrand Reinhold, 1974). Art for blind students.

4. GINSBERG, HERBERT, AND OPPER, SYLVIA. *Piaget's Theory of Intellectual Development: An Introduction* (Englewood Cliffs, N.J.: Prentice-Hall, 1969).

5. LENNAN, ROBERT K. "Report on a Program for Emotionally Disturbed Deaf Boys." *American Annals of the Deaf* 115 (1970): 469–473.

6. MALOTT, R. W., AND WHALEY, D. L. *Elementary Principles of Behavior*. Vols. 1, 2 (Kalamazoo, Mich.: Department of Psychology, Western Michigan University, 1968).

7. MEADOWS, KATHRYN, AND SCHLESINGER, HILDE S. "The Prevalence of Behavioral Problems in a Population of Deaf School Children." *American Annals of the Deaf* 116 (1971): 346–348.

8. MORROW, WILLIAM R., AND GOCHROS, HARVEY L. "Misconceptions Regarding Behavior Modification," *The Social Service Review* 44, No. 3 (Sept. 1970), p 293.

9. PATTERSON, G. R., AND GULLION, M. E. *Living With Children: New Methods for Parents and Teachers* (Champaign, Ill.: Research Press, Station A, 1968).

10. PIAGET, JEAN. *To Understand Is to Invent: The Future of Education* (New York: Viking Press, Grossman Publishers, 1975).

11. SKINNER, B. F., "Operant Behavior," *American Psychologist* 18 (1963): 503–515.

12. SCHRAG, PETER, AND DIVOKY, DIANE. *The Myth of the Hyperactive Child & Other Means of Child Control* (New York: Pantheon Books, 1975).

13. URQUHART, F. A. *The Monarch Butterfly* (Toronto, Canada: University of Toronto Press, 1960).

Appendix 2
Suggested Reading for Parents

1. BECKER, WESLEY C. *Parents Are Teachers* (Champaign, Ill.: Research Press, Station A, 1971).

2. BERNAL, M. E.; DURYEE, J. S.; PRUETT, H. L.; AND BURNS, B. J. "Behavior Modification and the Brat Syndrome," *Journal of Consulting and Clinical Psychology* 32 (1968): 447–455.

3. DANIELS, LLOYD K., ed. *Management of Child Behavior Problems at School and at Home* (Springfield, Ill.: Charles C. Thomas, 1974).

4. ERICKSON, RUTH RODGERS, AND ERICKSON, EDSEL. *How to Diagnose and Correct Your Child's Reading Problem* (Holmes Beach, Fla.: Teaching and Learning Publications, 1975).

5. LINDSELY, O. R. "An Experiment with Parents Handling Behavior at Home," *Johnstone Bulletin* (Johnstone Training Center, Bordertown, N.J. 9 (1966): 27–36.

6. PATTERSON, GERALD R. *Families* (Champaign, Ill.: Research Press, Station A., 1973).

7. PATTERSON, GERALD R., AND GUILLION, M. ELIZABETH. *Living with Children* (Champaign, Ill.: Research Press, 1973).

8. SHEPPARD, WILLIAM C. *Teaching Social Behavior to Young Children* (Champaign, Ill.: Research Press, 1973).

9. SMITH, J. M., AND SMITH, D.E.P. *Child Management: A Program for Parents* (Ann Arbor, Mich.: Ann Arbor Publishers, 1966).

10. SCHRAG, PETER, AND DIVOKY, DIANE. *The Myth of the Hyperactive Child & Other Means of Child Control* (New York: Pantheon Books, 1975).

11. WAGNER, M. K. "Parent Therapists: An Operant Conditioning Method." *Mental Hygiene* 52 (1968): 452–455.

12. WAHLER, R. G.; WINKEL, G. H.; PETERSON, R. E.; AND MORRISON, D. C. "Mothers as Behavior Therapists for Their Own Children." *Behaviour Research and Therapy* 3 (1965): 113–124.

13. WOLF, BERNARD. *Don't Feel Sorry for Paul* (New York: J. P. Lippincott, 1974).

Bibliography

1. AYLLON, TEODORA, AND AXRIN, NATHAN. *The Token Economy,* Appleton-Crofts Century Psychology Series (New York: Meredith Corp., 1968).

2. FERNALD, GRACE. *Remedial Techniques in Basic School Subjects* (New York: McGraw-Hill, 1943).

3. GREENFELD, JOSH. *A Child Called Noah* (New York: Warner Paperback Library, 1973).

4. HAEUSSERMANN, ELSE. *Developmental Potential of Preschool Children* (New York: Grune and Stratton, 1958).

5. KIRK, SAMUEL A. *Educating Exceptional Children* (New York: Houghton-Mifflin, 1972).

6. MALOTT, R. W., AND WHALEY, D. L. *Elementary Principles of Behavior,* Vols. 1, 2 (Kalamazoo, Mich.: Department of Psychology, Western Michigan University, 1968).

7. SHOSTROM, EVERETT L. *Man, the Manipulator* (New York: Abingdon Press, 1967).

8. ROBERTS, PAUL. *Understanding English* (New York: Harper & Row, 1958).

9. URQUHART, F. A. *The Monarch Butterfly* (Toronto, Canada: University of Toronto Press, 1960).

10. WOLF, BERNARD. *Don't Feel Sorry for Paul* (New York: J. P. Lippincott, 1974).

Index

Actualizers vs. manipulators, 28
Aggressive behavior, 37–44
Andersen, Hans Christian, 140
Autism, 48–52
Ayllon, Teodoro, 127
Azrin, Nathan, 127

Behavior(s), 3–4
    aggressive, 37–44
    consistency in, 30–31
    deceptive, 57–64
    evaluation of, 115–16
    goals, 19
    passive, 47-54
    stemming from physical
            impairment, 67–76
Blindisms, 71, 130
Blindness, 70–72
Brain damage, 75
Browne, Sir Thomas, 122
Bulletin boards, 10–11
Bullying, 38–40

Callum, Albert, 8
Cerebral palsy, 75–76
Cheating, 61–63
Classrooms, 9–12
    democracy in, 29
    environment of, 10, 12
    location of, 9
    token economy in, 124–37
Class store, 132–33
Clowning, 37–38
Clumsiness, 53–54
Consistency, 30–31

Daily check sheets, 19–22, 115
    from bus driver, 118
    at home, 107–8, 117–18
Deceptive behavior, 57–64
Deficiencies, in reading and spelling,
        79–80

de Maupassant, Guy, 46
Desk arrangement, 12
Discipline, 25–34
Double standards, 108–9

Educable mental impairment, 72–73
Emotional impairment, 3–4, 33
    and reading deficiencies, 79–80
Enright, Elizabeth, 102
Environment, 10, 103, 108–9
Epilepsy, 74–75
Exhibitionism, 37

Family, communication with, 103–9
Fernald, Grace, 85–89
Fines, 130–31
Follow-up, after screening out, 146
Fuller, R. Buckminster, 92

Goals, 15–22
    recording of, 16
    short-term, 17–18
    working for, 18–19
Grades, 113–15
Greenfeld, Josh, 48–49

Haeussermann, Dr. Else, 49
Haley, Alex, 78
Hawkins, Robert P., 83, 127, 141
Hayes, J. Eric, 83
Hearing impairment, 69
Hostility, 41–42
Huitema, Bradley E., 141
Hyperactivity, 73–74

Individual tutoring, 81, 88
I.Q. score, 72, 73

Kalamazoo Gazette, 2
Kirk, Samuel A., 70

Landers, Ann, 2
Learning disability, 72

Lewis, Richard, 36

Magruder, Jeb Stuart, 56
Malcolm X, 78
Manipulators vs. actualizers, 28
Masturbation, 53
Mathematics, 93–96
Mental impairment, 72–73
Modeling, 32
Moliere, 56
Moorman, Chick, 62–63
Mosier, Doris
    and J. J. Vaal, Jr., 40

Nagging, 41
New math, 94

Objectivity, for physically-impaired
    child, 67–69

Parents
    conferences with, 107
    cooperative, 103–4
    hostile, 104–7
    reports from, 107–8, 117–18
    reports to, 116–17
Partial visual impairment, 71–72
Passive behaviors, 47–54
Pathological lying, 58–59
Pepys, Samuel, 24
Phasing out, 141–45
    check sheets during, 118–19
    incremental steps during, 142–43
    prerequisites to, 143–45
    rewards during, 134
    of tokens, 131–32
Physical impairment, 67–76
Principle of controlled freedom, 31–32
Psychological tool, 124
Pushkin, 14

Reading
    deficiencies in, 79–80
    instruction in, 81–83
Reciprocal teaching, 83, 95

Remediation, 80
Reports, 21, 116–17. See also
        Daily check sheets
Rewards, 132–34
    privileges as, 132–33
    selecting, 132
Roberts, Paul, 83–84
Rogers, Will, 4
Role playing, 32–33
Rules, 29–30
    for students, 29–30
    for teacher, 30

Schizophrenia, 48
School Adjustment Program
        (Kalamazoo,
        Michigan), 126
Schoolwork, as therapy, 4–5
Science, 96–98
Screening out, 141, 145–46
Self-discipline, 25–27, 33, 137
Shikoski, Thomas I., 141
Shostrom, Everett L., 28
Skinner, B. F., 112
Social studies, 98–99
Special education, 3, 103, 113–14,
        141, 144
Speech impairment, 69–70
Spelling
    deficiencies in, 79–80
    and writing, 83–89
Stealing, 59–60
Student conferences, 16
Stuttering, 54

Tattling, 40–41
Teacher's aide, 9–10
Teacher-therapist
    main task of, 4
    and parents, 103–7
    and physically impaired, 67, 76
    qualities of, 5
    self-discipline for, 33–34
Teaching
    double standards, 108–9

math, science, and social
        studies, 93–99
reading, spelling, and
        writing, 79–89
self-discipline, 25–27, 137
Teaching aids, 10–12
Teasing, 38–40
Temper tantrums, 42-44
Therapy, school work as, 4–5
Token economy, 123–137
    advantages of, 136–37
    criticisms of, 125
    definition of, in the
            classroom, 124–25
    risks of, 134–36
Tokens, 126–32
    phasing out of, 131–32
    rules for using, 127–30

Trust, developing, 64

UCLA Clinic School for Non-Readers
        at Los Angeles, 85
Untruthfulness, 57-58
Urquhart, F. A., 96

Vaal, Jr., J. J.
    and Doris Mosier, 40

Withdrawal, 47–48
Wolf, Bernard, 66, 76
Word box, 86
Word strips, 85–86
Writing, 83-89

Zuckerman, Edward, 36